PERSONAL
RELIGION
AMONG THE
GREEKS

ANDRÉ-JEAN FESTUGIÈRE, O.P.

UNIVERSITY OF CALIFORNIA PRESS

BERKELEY AND LOS ANGELES · MCMLIV

University of California Press
Berkeley and Los Angeles
California

Cambridge University Press
London, England

L. C. Catalog Card No. 53-11234
Printed in the United States of America

SERVANT OF ISIS
(Louvre: bronze 4165)

GVERNERO

JAEGER

· S ·

ΈΜΝΗΣΘΗΝ Δ' ΌΣΣΑΚΙΣ ᾽ΑΜΦΟΤΕΡΟΙ

ῬΉΛΙΟΝ ᾽ΕΝ ΛΕΣΧΗΙ ΚΑΤΕΔΎΣΑΜΕΝ

PREFACE

THE EIGHT chapters of this book are substantially the lectures given by me on the Sather Foundation at the University of California, Berkeley, in the autumn of 1952.

They provide, of course, only glimpses of a very suggestive topic which is sometimes thrown into the shadows in the histories of Greek religion. There is a tendency in our time either to emphasize the civic part of this religion because it is immediately manifest or to take the Greek gods as they come to us in consequence of a long tradition, namely, as aesthetic symbols or fictions of poetic imagination. But, at least till the fourth century before our era, the Gods of Greece were not fictions; they were living beings who could view the actions of mortals, listen to their prayers, concede or reject their petitions. And if this is so, granted a certain uniformity in the human mind, we should expect *a priori* to find in Greece some personal religion. In fact we do find it already in Homer, and already there it is of a very fine quality. When Achilles prays to Zeus before sending Patroclus to the battle (*Iliad* XVI 236 ff.), when Diomedes prays to Athena after being wounded by Pandarus (*Iliad* V 115 ff.), when Sappho in one of her sad moods prays to Aphrodite (*Fr.* 1, Diehl), they do not say as does Chryses the priest (*Iliad* I 37 ff.), "If ever in the past I gave you 'such and such good things,' now you also must give me 'this.'" They say, "If ever in the past you listened to my prayer, now also you must listen to me." This, if anything, is personal religion. It is a religion of deep friendship. The devotee does not place his confidence in the respect he has shown to the god; he places it in the god's friendliness.

I would have liked to give more examples than I have here collected of this gentle and naïve faith of the archaic and classic periods. I would have liked in particular to show how sincere is the devotion of Ion to Apollo, of the Lydian women to Dionysus. But since the topic is somewhat new, I have thought it more expedient to try to present a more general survey. If this book has any value, wiser men will come and pursue the idea, and this will be my best reward.

It remains, and it is indeed a pleasure, to acknowledge the many obligations I have contracted in the preparation of this book. First, to the University of California, which invited me to become Sather professor, and to its friendly department of Classics. Then, to Milman and Barbara Parry, who translated my manuscript from the original French; to Professor A. D. Nock of Harvard University, who revised it and made valuable suggestions; to Professor I. M. Linforth of the University of California, who favored me with several acute critical observations. Also, to the Fathers and Brothers of Saint Albert's College, who were helpful to me in so many ways, and especially to the Very Rev. B. M. Blank, O.P., and the Very Rev. J. Fulton, O.P., my hosts during my stay in California. And to M. Charbonneaux, for the photograph of a bronze in the Louvre which is reproduced as a frontispiece to the book. Nor must I allow myself to forget Mr. Harold A. Small and Professor Emeritus W. H. Alexander, of the University of California Press, to whose skill and care this volume ultimately owes so much.

A.-J.F.

Oakland, California
December, 1952

CONTENTS

I

The Two Currents in
Personal Religion

Popular Piety: Hippolytus and Artemis

RELIGION might perhaps be defined, very generally, as belief in a fourth dimension—a dimension which takes us out of material space, where everything changes, disorder reigns, and we are lonely and unhappy, to attain *something which is*, a Being who exists absolutely, in all perfection and splendor. To feel that we are bound to that Being, that we are dependent on Him, to aspire to find Him, to hunger and thirst after Him: that is the religious sense.

The religious man is he who sees things here below, and at the same time sees them not—for he perceives other things behind the appearances of this earth, things more real, more in harmony with his heart; other things which are known to him, for they seem to be of his true country, his real place, whereas things earthly are foreign or hostile to him.

The religious man is he who senses, beyond earthly things, a Presence, and who needs to feel that Presence. For, let him cease to feel it, and all is emptiness, the world is no more than a desert in which he is lost.

Such feeling, needless to say, is personal in its nature. There is no true religion except that which is personal. True religion is, first of all, closeness to God. Every religious ceremony is but empty make-believe if the faithful who participate in it do not feel that thirst for the Absolute, that anxious desire to enter into personal contact with the mysterious Being who is hidden behind appearances.

Now, the question which I am here to put before you is this: was that personal religion known to the Greeks?

1

Yes, for to begin with there is Plato, Plato whose religious thought colored the spirituality of all the centuries to come. Now Plato is just the man who hungers and thirsts after the Absolute. He wants to attain to a Beauty which is not beautiful merely under one aspect, nor beautiful only at a given moment, but which is always and absolutely beautiful. And since, as we shall show, this Beauty is but one of the names of the supreme reality, what Plato in truth strives to attain is God himself. He does need to feel himself united to God. And after him, many of those impelled by the same need will be found to seek God in the ways first set forth by him.

But Plato is not an isolated prodigy in the history of Greek religion. If he left his mark on all that came after, he himself bears the mark of all that went before.

Here we must make some distinctions which will help toward a better understanding of the problem. First, the distinction between what I shall call *popular piety* and *reflective piety*. Next, the distinction between what belongs to the individual and what belongs to the group.

1) The highest form of religion is that which unites us with the very being of God. And since that being is altogether immaterial, remote from the world of sense, the perception, or awareness, that we have of Him is equally free from any material or sensual representation. Such a union is, by definition, an inner phenomenon; to attain it there is no need of outward ceremony, or of sacrifice or vocal prayers. It consists of an assimilation of the most immaterial part of ourselves to the principle of all that exists. Already Plato called it ὁμοίωσις θεῷ, "becoming like God."

But not all men are capable of that union. To begin with, we must recognize that there are men who are almost entirely a-religious. Then, even among religious men, many are incapable of that entirely pure and immaterial union. They have the awareness of God, but, to reach him, they must have intermediaries: divine or deified beings whom one can see, touch, whose image one can make, to whom one can appeal as to beings like unto ourselves, who differ from us only in that they are better and stronger. Union with such beings may be true and deep, may even become mystical union. Let us take an example. No one will deny that the Middle Ages in Europe were among the most religious in the history of the world. Now there were undoubtedly in the Middle Ages mystics who sought God directly, who sought to penetrate the divine essence and to lose themselves in an ineffable union in that Essence: such were St. Thomas, St. Bonaventure, Meister Eckhart. But there were other mystics, all of whose loving devotion was concentrated on visible, perceptible objects, akin to ourselves, Jesus in his humanity, Our Lady, and the Saints: and such was St. Francis of Assisi, and, generally speaking, the Franciscan School. And alongside these mystics, there were any number of good men, sincerely and deeply religious, who were content to spend long hours in contemplation before a statue of the Virgin or the infant Jesus, or the crucified Christ. That also was personal religion, very elevated and very genuine.

2) Let us go on to the second distinction, between what belongs to the individual and what belongs to the group.

The first form of union with God, union with the divine Essence, does not require that people gather together to pray. The hermit in his desert, the prisoner in his cell, may be invaded by God, may be absorbed in God. Mysticism is something which cannot be shared. One should always mistrust manifestations of mystical exaltation where whole crowds go into a trance. On the other hand, this form of union with God is not necessarily incompatible with public worship. It would be absurd to think that, because others worship near you, you are incapable of worshiping. Better yet, there is in public worship a kind of official homage paid to God, which can nourish private devotion and give it new life.

What I have just said is even more true when public veneration is being directed toward those intermediaries of whom we were speaking. Some among you have, perhaps, been present at the ceremonies in honor of the Virgin at Lourdes. When a whole crowd has its eyes fixed on the statue of Our Lady, when a whole crowd beseeches her, it happens that even those who do not believe are moved by that fervor, and then, sometimes, religious feeling is awakened in their hearts, and they in their turn stammer out a prayer. Would this be possible if they had not felt around them a great tide of personal piety, individual piety multiplied by the number of persons who engaged in heartfelt prayer?

Let us apply these distinctions to the problem of the personal religion of the Greeks and start with popular devotion and reflective piety.

1) Traditional religion in Greece, and, consequently, popular devotion, was mainly directed toward national gods, each of whom was the recognized protector of a certain city: Athena at Athens, Demeter at Eleusis, Hera at Argos, Apollo at Cyrene, Artemis at Ephesus, and so forth. For many reasons, however, reasons related partly to the Indo-European invasions of Greece and to the resultant intermingling with native populations, partly to the conquests of this city or that and to local synoecisms, partly to the first attempts at theological systematization, every Greek city honored, alongside its particular deity, other gods and goddesses: a kind of pantheon. The special deity of a given city usually acquired several attributes, since he or she had to satisfy the manifold needs of the social group. But that same god or goddess, considered as a member of the Olympian group, assumed a more distinct personality which set him or her apart from the others. Thus each of the Olympians was differentiated by particular qualities or functions, and popular devotion, collective or individual, could thenceforth be directed toward this or that god or goddess, because of special affinities between that god and the worshiper. It follows, then, that certain nuances were possible in popular worship; it made a difference whether prayers were addressed to the main and official deity of the city, or to other Olympian gods.[1] Here again we may make a comparison with the Middle Ages. That a city should consider the Virgin or a saint as its official patron was

---

[1] For notes, see pages 143–176 below.

common practice in medieval times: *Sena vetus civitas Mariae,*
one reads on the gates of Sienna. And the suburbs of Saint-Ouen
and Saint-Denis, now swallowed up in the immense territory of
Paris, still bear the names of the saints especially honored by
the autonomous little cities which Saint-Ouen and Saint-Denis
used to be. It is nevertheless quite evident that, in addition to a
local Virgin or regional saints, the Siennese or the inhabitants
of Saint-Denis could honor and pray to other heavenly patrons,
according to individual preferences.

On the other hand, there existed in Greece reflective piety.
The Greeks, or at least the most cultivated among them, believed in God. I say *God* with intention: the principle of the
order of things and of the course of human affairs, the guarantor
of justice and consequently the foundation of social ethics, the
Being endowed with every perfection. The idea of God as the
principle of nature appeared in Greece with the Pre-Socratics,
as Professor Jaeger has reminded us quite recently in his fine
book.[2] But the idea of God as guarantor of justice, and First
Cause of all the events of human life, is yet older. It is found
first in Hesiod, then in Pindar,[3] and with incomparable splendor
in Aeschylus. The purifying of the idea of God did not begin
with Plato. Deeply religious poets like Pindar, Aeschylus, and
in my opinion Euripides also, had already conceived a very high
and pure idea of the divine.

2) Let us now examine what is concerned in the distinction in
Greece between what belongs to the individual and what belongs to the group.

The God of inner devotion, the God of Hesiod, of the tragedians and the philosophers, was never the object of public
worship in Greece. Devotion to that God always remained a
private affair: such veneration was characteristic of cultivated
pagans, who had reflected on the great problems of life and had
arrived at a purer concept of the Divinity, either because they
themselves had philosophic souls, or because they had learned
from philosophers. From that time on, union with God, in the
sense of inner devotion, has always been personal in character.

Plato, as I have said, played a decisive role in the history of that devotion. That does not mean that he was the first in Greece to adore the supreme God. After all, it would be *a priori* remarkable that a people as gifted as the Greeks should have waited centuries to know the thirst for the Eternal, the Absolute. I shall set before you in my next chapter the presentiments of this aspiration toward God in the Greeks of the Classical Age.

The problem is more complex when one considers traditional religion.

Seen from without, traditional Greek religion has all the marks of a social phenomenon, a thing which concerns the state. Temples are dedicated to the civic gods. Priests are civic magistrates. On certain days all the citizens, in a body, men, women, and children, gather before the temple for a solemn sacrifice. The hymns then sung in honor of the god, the prayers addressed to him, have an official character: it is a matter of obtaining the god's favor for the prosperity and well-being of the entire people. Athena is the goddess of Athens, of the Athenians considered as a social entity, before being the goddess of the Athenian as a private individual.

Nevertheless, we should be mistaken if we believed that even the official deity of a city, such as Athena at Athens, received no more than purely civic homage. We possess, for the sixth and fifth centuries B.C., a long series of private dedications to Athena in which the piety of individual Athenians is often expressed with charm and feeling.[4] A new study of these *anathemata* from the point of view of personal religion would not be out of place. I should like to remind you also of the beautiful metope of the treasury of the Athenians at Delphi, on which young Theseus looks the goddess full in the face and from that look gathers strength. Now, Theseus is the symbol of the Ephebi, and Athena, warrior goddess, goddess bearing the helmet and lance, was a kind of elder sister for the ephebus, and, generally speaking, for the young hero exposed to the risks of combat and the hazards of life. That is a very ancient concept. As early as the *Iliad*, we see that there is an intimate, personal bond between Athena and Achilles, the purest type of the Greek hero. In the *Odyssey*, Athena is, as you know, the guardian and adviser of Telemachus. On Dorian soil, we have the admirable metope of Olympia where Athena encourages the Dorian hero Herakles.

Likewise it would be absurd to suppose that all those who participated in the Eleusinian Mysteries saw in them only a kind of external gesture or act which mechanically assured happiness here below and after death. John Burnet, who had nothing of the mystic in him, writes quite amusingly: "The candidate for initiation was only asked to sacrifice his pig. That was enough." But Aristotle more correctly says: "The candidate did not have to learn (μαθεῖν), but to experience (παθεῖν), something, and to come to be in a certain state of mind, provided, that is to say, that he was fit for that."[5] Of course, all were not fit. In the words of the Orphic saying, taken up by Plato, "Many wear the thyrsus, but there are few bacchants."[6] Yet true bacchants must have existed, then as today. There is an appropriate image in the works of St. Catherine of Sienna. Of those who take part in a procession, she says, some carry big tapers, others small ones. And the flame of those tapers is in proportion to their size. So it is with our hearts: the more intense the desire, the stronger the flame which God imparts. We may be sure that Aeschylus, at least, carried a big taper:

> Demeter, thou who feedest all my thought,
> Grant me but worthiness to worship thee.[7]

There could, then, be personal devotion toward even the civic gods. We also possess archaeological and literary evidence of personal devotion toward the Olympians, or toward some lesser god or local hero to whom, here or there, someone felt attached in a special manner. The most famous literary evidence is perhaps the *Hippolytus* of Euripides, of which I shall have something to say presently. But let us first discuss briefly the archaeological documents. They are of two kinds and concern religion in the countryside and religion in the home.

In certain French provinces, such as Brittany or Savoy, one

still finds, along the road, or on a mountaintop, or by the sea-shore, little chapels of the Virgin or of a saint, which popular devotion decks with ex-votos and flowers. Now the worshiper who comes there, offering a gift, comes as a private individual. No one sees him; it is not custom which brings him; he is not obliged to go there, as, for example, he feels himself obliged to go to Mass in his village because everybody else does. No, he comes to the wayside chapel to suit himself, because he wants to pray, to converse heart to heart with the good Virgin or the saint.

So in reading Pausanias one learns that at every step of his travels in Greece during the second century of our era, he saw such little rustic shrines, often abandoned, sometimes even in ruins, which had once, however, been living places of prayer for the humble folk of the region. In his *Greek Popular Religion*,[8] Nilsson has emphasized just that rustic aspect of Greek religion, and has shown what it means for personal piety. At this rural chapel the peasant on his way to town to sell his vegetables would pause, and so too the shepherd leading his flocks. They offered to the god, or the local hero, some slight gift. In return, they expected from him protection for themselves, for their modest family life, for their crops or their animals. We should be very wrong to consider this offering, with what it implied by way of return from the god, as merely an exchange or a bargain. It could have been that, no doubt, and it is thus that Euthyphro in Plato defines religion.[9] But the soothsayer Euthyphro is not a religious man. The religious man naturally relies upon the god. He gives him little presents because he loves him, and because the god is strong and good, because he has confidence in him, he expects from him, quite naturally, help and protection. That is no more a bargain than that which exists between a child and his parents, between a younger friend and an older one. What is more, even without an offering, the prayer of the passer-by is granted. Listen to this pretty epigram of the Macedonian Addaeus, a real "country gentleman," as Mackail calls him, in the beginning of the fourth century: "If thou pass by the hero, and he is called Philopragmon ['fond of business'] who lies by the crossroads in front of Potidaea, tell him to what work thou leadest thy feet; straightway will he, being by thee, make thy business easy."[10]

Sometimes the sight of a tall and beautiful tree caused simple people to believe that a god inhabited it. Anything which gave the impression of singular beauty and strength appeared at once to the Greeks to be impregnated with the divine. You all have in mind the famous passage in the *Phaedrus*[11] where, in the beginning of the dialogue, Socrates and his young friend following barefoot the course of the Ilissos come to an enormous plane tree. There they find a stream, a slope of fresh grass, on which they can stretch out in the shade amid the sounds of leaves, water, and cicadas. So delightful a place is, for the ancient, a sacred place, a place to pray. And so it is by a prayer that the *Phaedrus* ends: "O beloved Pan and all ye other gods of this place, grant to me that I be made beautiful in my soul within, and that all external possessions be in harmony with my inner man."[12]

Another feature of Greek religion which could, which must have given rise to feelings of personal piety was domestic religion. This aspect too has been brought out by Nilsson in his discussion of Zeus Ktesios, who watches over family possessions, and Zeus Philios of the symposium.[13] The *deisidaimon* of Theophrastus, who is not "superstitious" in our modern sense, but "a man overscrupulous in the cult he pays the gods," possesses in his home a divine image which he decks on certain days and to which he offers gifts.[14] The same Theophrastus tells, apropos of household religion, the following anecdote: A rich citizen of Magnesia on the Maeander came one day to Delphi. He was accustomed to perform each year abundant and splendid sacrifices. Having then completed a hecatomb at Delphi, he asked the oracle who was the most pious of men. The Pythia answered that Clearchus, a poor inhabitant of Methydrium in Arcadia, was the most pious. The Magnesian then went to Clearchus and questioned him: "How do you honor the gods?" Clearchus re-

Who is the most pious?

plied: "I fulfill all my religious duties to the letter. I sacrifice joyously at the established times, each month at the new moon, offering wreaths and adorning Hermes, Hecate, and the other divine images which my ancestors bequeathed me, honoring them by an oblation of incense, barley, and little cakes."[1]

To the question which we have been asking ourselves from the beginning, we can now give the answer: Yes; the Greeks did have a personal religion, in the form both of popular and of reflective piety.

It is my present purpose to give you some examples of personal religion in Greece, examples of the two aspects which we have defined. Because certain features of the Hellenistic Age—notably the decline of the city-state and the prevailing influence of Plato—favored the growth of personal religion, my examples will be chosen principally from the Hellenistic and Greco-Roman periods. In two chapters I shall examine two instances of piety in its popular, affective form: of Lucius toward Isis, and of Aristides toward Asclepius. Then we shall study two main aspects of reflective piety: union with the Cosmic God, and union with the pure divine essence beyond the limits of this world. However—and let me stress this point,—these forms of personal religion after Alexander do not constitute a novelty in Greece. Nothing changes so completely in the nature of man when deep-seated impulses are in question. Even before Plato, certain Greeks aspired to penetrate the mystery of God. And the single example of Hippolytus would suffice to convince us that the popular religion brought to flower the most exquisite sentiments of devotion to the Olympians.

⟡   ⟡   ⟡

Who, then, is Hippolytus? To understand what Euripides wished to express in the play of that name, and to grasp the originality of the character that he created, we must examine the starting point of the poet, which was a marriage song of the maidens of Troezen.[16] Before entering into marriage and losing their virginity, the maidens of Troezen went to lay a lock of their hair before the god or hero Hippolytus in his sanctuary:

For yokeless maids before their bridal night
Shall shear for thee their tresses;[17]

(1425 f.)

while with their companions they sang a hymn which told how
this virgin hero died for his chastity's sake:

And virgins' thoughts in music evermore
Turn toward thee, and praise thee in the Song
Of Phaedra's far-famed love and thy great wrong.

(1428–1430)

The essential quality of Hippolytus—his purity—was therefore contained in the tradition; so also was the legend of
Phaedra, which stresses his purity. Other details too were furnished in advance. Hippolytus is the son of an Amazon, one of
those warrior women who live far from men and honor Ares
and Artemis; he is, by Theseus, the great-grandson of the
"chaste" Pittheus.[18] For the Greek, who readily transposed
human feelings onto a mythological plane, the purity of Hippolytus necessarily made of him the friend of Artemis and the
enemy of Aphrodite, so that the human drama was but a ter-
restrial prolongation of an ancient and constant enmity between
those two dwellers on Olympus.

Starting from these simple and somewhat crude data provided
him by legend and tradition, Euripides has made them undergo
mysterious transmutations, and what emerges from the crucible
is one of the most astonishing characters in Greek tragedy—so
astonishing, in fact, that the judgments one may make about
him are necessarily subjective. So then shall mine be. The illus-
trious Wilamowitz[19] depicts Hippolytus in one word: he is
ἀνεπαφρόδιτος, that is to say, without the graces of Aphrodite,
without any kind of charm, incapable of loving, and not feeling
the need to be loved. He is a proud man, a pure egoist, sufficient
unto himself. I hasten to tell you that my opinion is very different. In the first place, if there were nothing admirable about
Hippolytus, how could Phaedra, upon a mere glance, have been
seized with such passionate love for him (v. 27)? But this

obvious objection is only a negative one. It is enough to read the exquisite prayer of the opening to sense the charm of Hippolytus and to discern the source of this charm (vv. 73 ff.):

> To thee this wreathèd garland, from a green
> And virgin meadow bear I, O my Queen,
> Where never shepherd leads his grazing ewes
> Nor scythe has touched. Only the river dews
> Gleam, and the spring bee sings, and in the glade
> Hath Solitude her mystic garden made.
> No evil hand may cull it: only he
> Whose heart hath known the heart of Purity,
> Unlearned of man, and true whate'er befall.
> Take therefore from pure hands this coronal,
> O mistress loved, thy golden hair to twine.
> For, sole of living men, this grace is mine,
> To dwell with thee, and speak, and hear replies
> Of voice divine, though none may see thine eyes.
> Oh, keep me to the end in this same road!

One word dominates this page all instinct with poetry: *Aidos*, the Latin *pudor*, which is best rendered in English, I believe, by the word *modesty*. To feel the particular nuance of the word *Aidos*, we must remember that, in the moral ideas of the fifth-century Greeks, *aidos* is intimately bound up with that quality of *sophrosyne* which should be the distinguishing mark of the well-brought-up young man.[20] *Sophrosyne* has no equivalent in modern languages: it is the quality of him whose soul is healthy, in whom all is well-ordered, who consequently does not abandon himself either to immoderate pride or to degrading passions. *Aidos* is, then, the feeling which makes us dread having to blush before others or before ourselves. Now what makes a young boy blush is above all a word or deed contrary to what is expected of him—a base or cowardly act.[21] You remember the scene in the *Charmides* of Plato where Socrates, at the gymnasium, meets the young Charmides who is presented to him as a model youth, *sophron*. Socrates then asks him what it means to be *sophron*. It means, Charmides first answers, to act in all things with pro-

priety and a composed bearing.[22] The definition is still too
vague. Socrates insists. Charmides thereupon gives a second
answer: "*Sophrosyne* is what makes one blush for certain things,
what makes one ashamed: in short, it is the same thing as
modesty."[23]

Charmides and Hippolytus are brothers, both very young,
and ready to blush at a trifle: life has not yet dulled that fresh
sensibility which is, as it were, the first blossoming of their soul.
That is what *aidos*, modesty, is. And then, by a marvelous
image, just as the character of Hippolytus recalls the velvety
brightness of a flower or a fruit still on the tree, so could one say,
with Euripides, of a field not yet mowed or trampled, a field
which has all its flowers, on which sparkles the morning dew,
that it is nourished by *aidos*.[24] Thus is created, from the beginning of the drama, an atmosphere of dawn or springtime which
gives us an almost physical sense of the hero's purity.

And now I think that we can understand Hippolytus. Let us
picture to ourselves a boy of about eighteen, well built and
handsome, sport-loving, of simple and upright character. He is
a virgin:

> And most in that one thing, where now thy mesh
> Would grip me, stainless quite! No woman's flesh
> Hath e'er this body touched. Of all such deed
> Naught wot I, save what things a man may read
> In pictures or hear spoke; nor am I fain,
> Being virgin-souled, to read or hear again.
>
> (1002–1006)

Certainly he has not yet felt any violent physical needs. He
takes pleasure in the company of lads his own age, with whom
he hunts in the forest or races his horses on the beach at Troezen.
Like many boys of his years, he has at the same time a fear,
even a certain physical horror, and a scorn, of womankind
(vv. 616 ff.). There is nothing morbid in his case. He is perfectly
normal. He simply does not yet think about love. Let me add
that he is truly pure, and does not practice Dorian love. When
Theseus, accusing his son of hypocrisy, indicates that he does not

find the latter's fine airs of virtue and purity convincing (vv. 949–951), Hippolytus voices a manly protest:

> Dost see
> This sunlight and this earth? I swear to thee
> There dwelleth not in these one man—deny
> All that thou wilt!—more pure of sin than I.
> Two things I know on earth: God's worship first;
> Next, to win friends about me, few, that thirst
> To hold them clean of all unrighteousness;
> Our rule doth curse the tempters, and no less
> Who yieldeth to the tempters.[26]
>
> (993–999)

All headmasters have known boys of this type. We should be very much mistaken in thinking that the fine flower of modesty was unknown to the ancients. One has only to reread the portrait of the well-bred Athenian in the agon of the *Clouds* of Aristophanes (vv. 961 ff.). So in the prologues to Plato's *Lysis*, *Charmides*, and *Protagoras* we find boys who blush easily, who have instinctively the feeling of *aidos*. But why look further than in Euripides himself? What is fresher, purer, more virginal than the beginning of the *Ion*, where Ion sings with so much naïve joy the merits of his god, Apollo?

Ion has given himself to Apollo. Hippolytus belongs to Artemis, the pure virgin huntress.

Out of a simple piece of legend Euripides has created a pearl of great price. The traditional bond between Hippolytus and Artemis was doubtless quite superficial. Artemis is the hunting goddess; she scours hill and thicket, there where the deer and boar hide themselves. Hippolytus was therefore shown as a young huntsman taken up with the chase after wild animals. This concrete and visible bond still subsists in Euripides' drama. When Hippolytus in his death-throes feels the presence of Artemis, he says to her: "Thy huntsman and thy servant lives no more" (v. 1397). But in the play that is but a secondary aspect of the union between the hero and the goddess.

Hippolytus has a real cult, true tenderness for Artemis. She is his Lady, in the language of a ·medieval knight. Better yet, she is for him what Our Lady was to a knight of the Middle Ages. "He is always in the Maid's train," Aphrodite complains in the prologue.[26] And Hippolytus himself declares:

> For sole of living men, this grace is mine,
> To dwell with thee, and speak, and hear replies . . .
> (vv. 84 f.)

Hippolytus speaks thus in the charming prayer uttered upon offering a wreath to Artemis. The following verse, which has not been noticed enough, leads us to say that this union was truly a mystical union:

> Of voice divine, though none may see thine eyes.
> (v. 86)

When Hippolytus utters this prayer, he is standing before the statue of Artemis. The stage setting represents the royal palace at Troezen. To the right and left of the central door stand statues of Artemis and Aphrodite, and before each statue an altar. Hippolytus, returning from the hunt with his companions, has laid a wreath upon the altar of Artemis, at the same time offering a prayer. How then can he say, in front of the statue, "Yet seeing not thy face"? It is because that Artemis who is the Lady of his thoughts, to whom he is forever speaking, and who answers him, is an inner image, more present to the eye of the soul than Hippolytus is to himself. But that is the very definition of love. The lover is emptied of himself; the being who lives in him is his beloved; he no longer sees or hears any other except that being; he is, as it were, possessed by her. Now when the beloved person is a divine being, we then speak of mystical love. For it is evident that there is here no question of physical union, but of soul with soul. The divinity is constantly present in the soul of the worshiper. The whole joy of the believer is in his consciousness of the presence of his god.

Euripides' entire play unfolds between two scenes in which mystical awareness of the divine is luminously evident. The first scene is that of the prayer, when, still moist with the dew of the woods, Hippolytus brings Artemis a garland. The last scene is that of his death. You are familiar with the circumstances of that death. Cursed by his father Theseus, who believes him guilty of adultery with Phaedra, Hippolytus, banished from Troezen, flees along the shore of the Saronic Gulf. Suddenly there rises from the sea a monstrous wild bull, which appears before the chariot of Hippolytus. His horses bolt; Hippolytus falls. Caught in the reins, he is dragged on the rocks. It is this poor, torn body which is carried back to Troezen by the attendants. Hippolytus, covered with blood, lies upon a bed brought from the palace. His father, whose eyes have been unsealed by Artemis, stands beside him. Hippolytus is consumed with pain: he has begged to be put to death. "O! For the blackness of Hades, the sleep of Necessity's night" (vv.1387 f.). But all at once he grows calm: he senses a celestial presence:

> HIPP. Ah!
>   O breath of heavenly fragrance! Though my pain
>   Burns, I can feel thee and find rest again.
>   The Goddess Artemis is with me here.
> ART. With thee and loving thee, poor sufferer!
> HIPP. Dost see me, Mistress, nearing my last sleep?
> ART. Aye, and would weep for thee, if Gods could weep.
> HIPP. Who now shall hunt with thee or hold thy quiver?
> ART. He dies; but my love cleaves to him for ever.
>   (1390–1400)

Here, too, I believe one may speak of mystical union. Hippolytus no longer sees or hears anything of the things of this world. He certainly does not behold the statue of the goddess. He cannot turn his head, can scarcely open his eyes. Yet at that terrible moment when he lies dying, without hope—for, although aware of his own innocence, he still does not know that Theseus, at last enlightened, bitterly repents having cursed him—at that moment, I say, the strength of his love for Artemis makes him believe that she is at his side. He will not die alone, nor in despair. She is there, he breathes in her perfume. His whole past comes back to him, his prayers, his simple confidence in the goddess, the little presents he used to offer her. "Thy huntsman and thy servant lives no more. . . . No more to drive thy steeds, to guard thy images." No more wreaths for Artemis. But the goddess replies: "No more, but thou art dear to me though dying."

Piety like that of Hippolytus was undoubtedly rare. Let us take two examples. The boys or young men whom Socrates meets in the gymnasium—Charmides, Lysis, the Hippocrates of the *Protagoras*—are very well bred: their manners are charming, and any family, any school, might well be proud of them. This perfect upbringing which they have received, their reserve, their docility, their gentility, justify us in believing that they practiced the traditional religion: on this score too they observed the good precepts they received at home. However, they do not give the impression of being truly religious. Their avid curiosity never lights upon questions of a religious nature. They do not question Socrates on this subject, and it is not as to spiritual directors that they turn with such eagerness to the Sophists. Nothing fresher, nothing more gracious, than the well-bred young men portrayed in the agon of the *Clouds* (vv. 961 ff.)—yet here, again, not the smallest allusion to any special devotion toward the gods.

Does this mean that personal piety was unknown at Athens in the time of Euripides? No, of course not, since Hippolytus exists. But it is doubtless true that such piety was rare, as it is today. Perhaps there is another reason to reckon with. Personal piety, when it is fervent and deep, is a peculiarity; it sets a man apart. The intensely religious man is wont to withdraw from the world in order to contemplate at leisure. He appears therefore to be solitary, odd, unsociable.[27] And nothing was more odious in classical Athens than unsociability. Call to mind the quarrel of Zethus with Amphion, the reproaches of Callicles to Socrates on the subject of the contemplative life. In every closed society such as that of Athens the first law of "savoir-vivre" is to behave like everybody else, not to set oneself apart. If Euripides was courageous enough to portray original characters, out of the common run, it is because, his biographers tell us, he was himself an "original," a recluse, and did not care a straw for what people would say. Thence it is possible that his tragedies give us a glimpse of certain aspects of the Athenian character which, without him, would have remained hidden from us.

II

The Two Currents in Personal Religion

Reflective Piety: The Quest of God

THAT FORM of union with the divinity which we examined in our first lecture we found to consist in an intimacy, at once simple and direct, between a man and his god. It in no way implied a disgust with the things of this world; it was not a flight to another sphere and another life. Hippolytus is perfectly happy in the here and now. Riding through the forest and along the sandy beach is bliss for him, and at his return there is joyous feasting with his comrades of the chase. Similarly, to take another example from Euripides, Ion, the delightful choirboy of Apollo, is perfectly happy in the Delphic temple. His wish is to remain there forever. When King Xuthus recognizes him as his son and wishes to take him to Athens, he at first refuses. Why should he trade the tranquil pleasures of a simple and innocent existence for the complications of the city and the anxieties of public life? The familiar relations of these young men with their beloved god or goddess do not constitute for them a deliverance; rather it is of the very essence of their present life; it is what makes that present life so full of charm. They are in fact creatures still young and unbruised by living. They have no complexities. They believe in happiness. And happiness for them is to be always with their celestial friends.

The other form of union with the divine which I should like to consider in this chapter presupposes on the contrary a profound disgust with life. Those who experience it have suffered. For them the earth is truly a vale of tears. As it is set forth in the *Theaetetus* (176AB), they are aware of the evil of this world.

19

The remedy they seek in flight, in a flight that will make them like unto God, φυγὴ ὁμοίωσις θεῷ.

Why this desire to become like unto the divine? In Plato, of course, the formula takes on a moral ring; one becomes like God by leading a pure and holy life with an enlightened mind. But this is, as so often with Plato, a transposition; Plato shifts to the plane of philosophy a preëxistent tendency which was not essentially an ethical principle. It was much more a fundamental aspiration of the human spirit. Above all our unhappiness, above this earth where men, like beasts, rend one another, where injustice reigns supreme and we live in an age of iron, the gods are perfectly happy.

This contrast between celestial bliss and earthly woe leads to several differing attitudes of the soul.

1) Sometimes it serves to prove the indifference of the gods to the misery of men. Up there, they pass their days in feasting and in the unbroken enjoyment of their beatitude; whereas we, down here, continue to suffer. The sense of this contrast is one of the most profound feelings in the human spirit. We have all of us felt it in hours of distress. How can God bear to see us thus suffering? And if he can bear it, then is he, in truth, God? Or are his plans hidden in such wise that we can never unveil their mystery? The whole of Greek tragedy is full of these questions.· Let us mention only the end of the *Trachiniae*. Heracles has died in unspeakable agony. Hyllus and his companions have borne out the corpse. Deianira has killed herself. There are left on the stage only the chorus and the unhappy Iole, the involuntary cause of this catastrophe. At this point the coryphaeus proclaims:

> And stay you not, Maiden, within the house.
> You have seen deaths great and strange,
> And many a sorrow of unknown shape,
> And nothing of these that is not Zeus.[1]

It is like the epitome of all the misfortune of man. Zeus, allpowerful and eternally happy, guides all things at his pleasure. Man can only endure. And all is said.

2) Sometimes, on the other hand, the contrast between the serenity of the gods and the turmoil of earthly things gives rise to an aspiration. Since the earth is bad, why not leave it? Why not fly to the place where the gods dwell, share their life and be happy like them? That is the original sense of this φυγή or flight to the gods, of this ὁμοίωσις or assimilation to the gods. It is a desire of escape, it is the homesickness for heaven, it is the aspiration to lose oneself, to pass from this world, into the unsounded depths of divine peace.

Assuredly, it is in Plato, and in all the varieties of Hellenistic mysticism derived from Plato, that this form of union was to find its most finished expression. But here again there are precursors in the classical age.

To begin with, the desire of escape is expressed in the Greek tragedians and especially in Euripides, sometimes through the mouth of a character, sometimes through that of the chorus, which in some way gives voice to the poet's own emotion. It cannot be said that this desire of escape is already a union with the divine. But it leads to that union. After all, one does not long for heaven if one is content with the things of earth. Conversely, the misery of earthly things is the incentive to the quest of another life, that of the gods.

In the second place, there is what we may call the mystery of Zeus.

On the one hand, Zeus is a just god. He who on earth is overwhelmed by the injustice of men can turn with confidence to the Highest; Zeus will hear his prayer (*Agam.* 48–59): "Shouting from an angry heart the cry for a mighty war, like vultures that, in extreme (?) grief for their children, high above their bed circle round and round, rowing with all the oars of their wings, having lost the couch-keeping labor they had spent over their nestlings; but one in the height, Apollo it may be, or Pan or Zeus, hearing the shrill cry of the birds' lament, and ⟨feeling great compassion for⟩ the denizens in his realm, sends on the transgressors her who brings punishment, though late, Erinys."[2]

On the other hand, daily experience teaches us that God does not hear every prayer. Moreover, not only does God appear ruthless, but it seems at times that the happiness of men angers the gods, and that they take a sort of pleasure in watching us suffer. What, then, *are* the ways of Zeus? And how are we to penetrate this mystery of suffering?

Such are the problems which I should like to consider next. They are old problems, and after so many fine studies that have been made on Greek tragedy, I do not pretend to tell you things entirely new. However, I could not omit treatment of this subject, in the first place because the mystery of Zeus, in Greek tragedy, throws much light on the personal religion of the Greeks in the Classical Age, and secondly because the efforts of the tragedians to penetrate this mystery already prefigure the great currents of Hellenistic mysticism.

THE DESIRE OF ESCAPE

In their celestial home the gods are eternally happy. "Having thus fulfilled her purpose, Athene went away to Olympus where evermore they say the seat of the gods stays sure: for the winds shake it not, nor is it wetted by rain, nor approached by any snow. All around stretches the cloudless firmament, and a white glory of sunlight is diffused about its walls. There the blessed gods are happy all their days."[3] And from this place of beatitude that is their habitation the gods regard with indifference the ills of man.

"Unhappy man!" cries Achilles upon the entrance of old Priam into his tent,

"Unhappy man! What mighty sorrows must thy spirit endure ...
But come, sit thee beside me upon my couch; let us alwise
Now put away our griefs, sore tho' we be plagued with affliction.
Truly there is no gain in distressful lamentation,
Since the eternal gods have assign'd to us unhappy mortals
Hardship enough, while they enjoy bliss idly without end."[4]

In like fashion, when she meets Demeter disguised as an old woman and seated at the Virgin's Well in Eleusis, Callidice, the daughter of King Celeus, says to her:

"Mother, we suffer as the gods ordain,
For we are men, and gods are mightier far."[5]

There would be no point in multiplying these citations. As far back as one may go in Greek literature, one finds this pessimistic sense of life. Again, from this pessimistic sense there may result, as we have said, a desire to escape. And this desire of escape in turn may assume two aspects.

First, there is escape by death. The idea of the "Second Best"[6] is a commonplace current throughout all Greek literature:

Never to have lived is best, ancient writers say;
Never to have drawn the breath of life, never to have
    looked into the eye of day.
The second best's a gay goodnight and quickly turn away.[7]

The alternative is the escape to a wonderland where the heroes beloved of the gods live a life similar to theirs. Man dreams of happiness. Seeing that this life is not a happy one, the ancient Greek moved happiness far away in space or far back in time. Thus were born the two related myths of the Golden Age and the Isles of the Blessed. The Golden Age recedes to the beginning of time, to old Cronos' reign, while the Isles of the Blessed lie at the furthest limits of the earth,[8] in that place of fantasy Sophocles describes:

Last peaks of the world, beyond all seas,
Wellsprings of night, and gleams of opened heaven,
The old garden of the Sun.[9]

Now when one reads on the one hand the description of the Golden Age in Hesiod,[10] and on the other the description of Elysium in the *Odyssey*[11] and in Pindar,[12] or again the description of the life of the Hyperboreans in Pindar[13] and in Sophocles,[14] and when one compares these representations with that of the life of the gods in Homer,[15] one observes that the same features are to be found in them all. The climate is the same: there is always resplendent light there, without clouds, or rain, or snow.[16]

Occupations are alike:[17] all the time joyous feasting and a life free from care.[18] Nor do the poets fail to speak in explicit terms of the similarity of the life of the Blessed and that of the gods: "In the Age of Gold," says Hesiod, "men lived as do the gods."[19] And Pindar says that the Blessed live a life without tears near to the glorious gods.[20]

It is, then, understandable that pitiful mankind should feel such yearning for the land of the gods. The theme of escape appears often in the works of the tragic poets, and especially in those of the most tender and most human of them, Euripides. When the misery of man in this world, born of some unmerited misfortune or of gnawing remorse, becomes too great for him, he dreams of wings that will somehow carry him away to a new life. Thus, the *Suppliants* of Aeschylus ask (792 ff.): "Wherefrom in the aether above could a high seat be given me, against which watery clouds turn into snow? Or some bare, smooth cliff that even goats cannot climb, some beetling vulture-crag that cannot be pointed at, so far is it withdrawing itself into proud seclusion?"[21] So, too, cries Creusa when she learns that Ion is not her son:

> "Oh, to flee on the wings of a bird
> Through the ocean of air, and from Hellas afar
> To the stars of the west!"[22]

"To the stars of the west," that is, to the setting sun, to the Garden of the Hesperides, to the westernmost point of the earth.

Usually, those are but fleeting sighs. In at least one place, however, in a chorus of the *Hippolytus*, the theme of flight is fully developed. As Wilamowitz has pointed out,[23] the song of the women of Troezen has no particular relation with the drama. It is true that, having been told by the nurse of Hippolytus' vehement refusal, Phaedra returns to the palace in despair and there is reason to fear a disaster. But in reality this disaster has little meaning for the women of Troezen: their sympathy is not for Phaedra, who is a stranger to them, but for the son of Theseus. Hence the theme of heavenward flight (742 ff.) is more

the expression of a secret wish of the poet than a dramatic re-
quirement of the play: "And to the apple-bearing strand of the
singing Maidens of the West I then would come, where the
Lord of the Sea no more to sailors grants a passage o'er the deep
dark main, finding there the heaven's holy bound upheld by
Atlas, where water from ambrosial founts wells up beside the
couch of Zeus within his halls, and holy Earth, the bounteous
mother, increaseth joy for the gods."[24]

Of course there will always be people to say that this is no
more than a poetical fancy to express the simple thought, "Oh,
could I but be as happy as the gods," without implying any idea
of a life lived *with* the gods. But in another instance of this
theme of escape I think that some sort of actual union with the
divine cannot be excluded from the meaning. When persecuted
together with their god Dionysus by Pentheus, king of Thebes,
the Lydian women also, who form the chorus of the *Bacchae*,
dream of a flight to a wondrous land (403–415). I venture the
following translation: "Oh that I could come unto Cyprus,
island of Aphrodite, which the Loves haunt, enchanters of the
mortal heart; to Paphos which the hundred-mouthed waters of
the foreign river fertilize without rain; to the land of fairest
Pieria, the holy slope of Olympus, where the Muses have their
abode. Thither, bring me thither, Bromios, Bromios, leader of
the Bacchantes, god of the Bacchic cry. There are the Graces,
there is Desire ($\pi\acute{o}\theta os$), there the Bacchae have the right to
serve Thee."

There are many traits in common between this chorus and
that from the *Hippolytus* quoted above. The Lydian women
wish to go to holy places, where the gods dwell—Aphrodite and
the Loves in Cyprus, the Muses and even all the gods (Olympus) in Pieria. And, as E. R. Dodds has pointed out in his commentary to the *Bacchae* (p. 117), "Cyprus represents the eastern
limit of the Greek world, as Olympus the northern limit."
Thus we find again the idea of peaceful and holy places at
the very edge of the Greek world. They are dream places.
This Cyprus is not the real Cyprus, but the island of Aphrodite

who is here, as Dodds says, "a symbol not of sensuality but of . . . happiness and liberation." This Pieria is not, or at least not only, the realm of Archelaos, but the traditional birthplace of the Muses. Moreover it is a Dionysiac country and, with Olympus thrown in, the abode of all the blessed gods. These holy places, holy because the gods dwell in them, are lands of pure delight. The Hesperides sing on the western strand and the Muses hymn their lays in Pieria; Cyprus is haunted by the Loves. It never rains in this imagined Paphos fertilized by the Nile; neither rain nor snow ever falls in heavenly Olympus. Now, what are the Lydian women of the *Bacchae* wanting to do in these dreamlands? ἐκεῖ δὲ βάκχαις θέμις ὀργιάζειν (415). They will worship their god in freedom and peace. This is precisely their idea of happiness: "O blessed is he who by happy favour knowing the sacraments of the gods, leads the life of holy service and is inwardly a member of God's company."[25]

Surely it cannot be denied that here, at least, we find the idea of a union with the divine. As Dodds, commenting on the preceding quotation, puts it, θιασεύεται ψυχάν refers "to the inward feeling of unity with the θίασος and through it with the god. (Verrall's 'congregationalises his soul' is the nearest English equivalent)."

THE MYSTERY OF ZEUS

ZEUS AND JUSTICE

In Greece as elsewhere, the first attribute of the divine is *power.* The gods are called the *kreissones*, that is, "the stronger ones." This attribute of power is essentially connected with the idea of God itself. For the idea of God is born in us of the fact that we are not the masters of the events of our lives; that no matter whether we prepare everything and arrange everything in the best possible manner beforehand, yet the final decision is not made by us, but by other beings stronger than we.

Thus these stronger ones order human affairs at their pleasure. But how do they order them? Human history, what we ourselves see about us, hardly suggests an optimistic view. The spectacle of the triumph of the evil and the suffering of the just man is only too familiar.

To tell oneself upon reflection, therefore, that either there are no gods or the ones that are take no interest in us, is quite normal. The young man in the *Laws* had already arrived at this conclusion, and many another with him. With this in mind, we cannot but feel our admiration strongly roused when we find that in the earliest times, since Homer and Hesiod, the great poetry of the Greeks expresses an unshakable confidence in the justice of Zeus. God is no longer God if he does not join the attribute of justice to that of omnipotence. Zeus *Xenios* protector of the guest, Zeus *Hikesios* protector of the suppliant, Zeus *Horkios* guardian of oaths, Zeus *Prostropaios* avenger of crime—all these are titles as ancient as those of power, Zeus *Basileus* (King), Zeus *Keraunios*, Wielder of Thunder, Zeus *Nephelegereta*, the Cloud-gatherer.

Whence comes this idea? It is an idea deeply rooted in the human heart that he who has done an ill must himself suffer a like ill. "An eye for an eye, and a tooth for a tooth."[26] "So has he done, so is he done by."[27] The progress lies precisely in that the primitive idea, or rather the instinct, of vengeance has been enriched by a moral sense. Zeus himself, the Most High, has taken the old adage for his own. "Ye mighty Fates, grant that with favor of Zeus the end may come upon the road where the Right also walks. *'For enmity of tongue let enmity of tongue be rendered'*: this is the loud cry of Justice as she is exacting her due. *'For a murderer's blow a murderer's blow shall be his payment. Let the doer be done by.'* Those are the words of a most ancient saying."[28]

The two significant words here are Διόθεν, "with favor of Zeus," and Δίκη, "justice." The ancient law of humanity is the *lex talionis*. For the ancient this was no abstract law. From the very blood of the victim and from the warm vapor that it gives forth, there arises and takes form a phantom, who will from then on follow the murderer all his days, wherever he may betake himself. It is the *Erinys*, the avenging demon. And not only does she dog the footsteps of the murderer; she likewise pursues the victim's nearest kin, as in the Orestes story, giving him no rest until he has avenged the crime. Such is the ancient law of the Fates. That is why the chorus of the *Choephoroe* begins its invocation with: Ὦ μεγάλαι Μοῖραι, "Ye mighty Fates!" Moreover, Zeus, the supreme god, has himself confirmed the ancient rule with his sovereign guarantee. Dike herself, Zeus's own daughter, demands that the guilty one be punished. All this constitutes a significant advance and a great deepening of personal religion; for a special bond is thereby established between the most powerful of the gods of heaven and all that is weakest on earth.

It is, after all, quite possible that the victim of an injustice may be of such low estate as to be entirely without the means of avenging himself. Or, in the case of a murder, it may happen that the victim has no descendants, or that those he has may be too weak to redress the wrong by themselves. Without Orestes, what would Electra do? Or finally the author of the crime may be a tyrant of such redoubtable power and prestige that anything but submission to him and to his acts would be out of the question. In such circumstances what is left? There is Zeus. Zeus becomes the champion of the oppressed. The less one can count on men, the more one can count on God. You all know the admirable parable told by Nathan in the story of David. In a city there lived a rich man and a poor man. The rich man had many flocks. The poor man had but one ewe lamb, which ate from his hand, slept at his side, and was to him as a daughter. But the rich man took from the poor man his ewe lamb, and slaughtered it. Such is the crime of David, who took the wife of his servant Uriah, and caused Uriah's death as well. Therefore the Lord says to David: "Behold, I will raise up evil against thee out of thine own house [and my curse is upon thee]."[29] An analogous idea appears and gains currency in Greece with the poem of Hesiod. The hawk says to the nightingale: "Where'er I take you, must you go: / And I shall eat, or set you free / Just as I choose."[30] But Zeus, who sees all things, is on guard, and always, sooner or later, he will punish the evildoer.[31] It would be no exaggeration to say that Hesiod's unwavering faith in the justice and the providence of Zeus has been one of the most powerful ferments of the Western conscience.

In what measure the idea of Zeus champion of justice and protector of the suppliant was a consolation to the average Greek, we cannot say. We do not know the prayers of the widow and the orphan. The tragic poets, however, and in particular Aeschylus, have given voice to popular sentiment. The first words of the first extant Greek tragedy, Aeschylus' *Suppliants*, are an invocation to Zeus Aphiktor: "May Zeus, protector of the suppliants, look in mercy upon this our band!"[32]

The whole drama, dominated by two great choral songs, is a long cry of frantic confidence in the god who rules on high and sees all things. "O king of kings, of the blessed the most blessed, of the perfect Powers the most perfect, all-happy Zeus, hear and grant that this shall be. Show thy just abomination of the lust of men and keep it from us."[33]

THE MYSTERY OF SUFFERING

The punishment of the evildoer most certainly answers a profound need of the human soul. But is all the problem of suffering no more than that? Deianira thought she did well. In order not to lose her husband's love, she sends him a magical robe. But the robe, it turns out, is covered with poison. In despair, Deianira hangs herself. Did she deserve her suffering? Heracles, all his labors ended, returns in joy to Thebes. He embraces his old father, his wife Megara, and his children. Hera, jealous of his happiness, sends him a demon of madness. In a fit, he kills his wife and children, and recovers from his frenzy only to realize the full extent of his misfortune. Of what crime had he been guilty, save that of being too happy? Was Hippolytus culpable? And Iphigenia? And the Trojan Women? And so with many other heroes and heroines of Greek tragedy? Truly, the punishment of the malefactor is but one aspect of the problem. There remains the suffering of the innocent. How are we to explain it?

The mystery of the suffering of the just man was deeply troubling to the Greek mind, and is always the most painful mystery to one who is religious. Let us consider it. God is happy; man suffers. If we say that our suffering is a deserved punishment sent by God, we can accept it. But if we are not aware of having sinned? If, on the contrary, we are aware of having always done, or at least of having tried to do, all that moral law demands of us? Then the action of the gods toward us becomes completely incomprehensible, and we are wandering in darkness.

Very early, the Greek set himself this problem. He found, successively, two answers. The first, which the Greeks themselves were quick to reject, is merely an extension of *suffering equals retribution*. The punishment of Zeus is sometimes slow to come: ὑστερόποινον πέμπει παραβᾶσιν Ἐρινύν, "Zeus sends on the transgressors her who brings punishment, though late, Erinys."[34] It may happen that Zeus does not punish the guilty one in his own person, but in that of his descendants. This is still just, according to those primitive conceptions whereby the significant social unit is not the individual, but the family. Thus the fault of the father is passed on to his children. And even if these children might appear to be innocent as individuals, they are collectively guilty, and therefore punished.

However, in Greece as in Judea,[35] moral conscience soon rebelled against this idea of hereditary penalty: "Father Zeus, I would it were the gods' pleasure . . . that whosoever did acts abominable and of intent, disdainfully, with no regard for the gods, should thereafter pay penalty *himself*, and the ill-doing of the father become no misfortune unto the children after him; and that such children of an unrighteous sire as act with righteous intent . . . , these should not pay requital for the transgression of a parent."[36]

So man is alone responsible for his own acts, and the problem remains untouched: why the suffering of the innocent?

Faced with such a problem, a man who is deeply religious, who believes in God, and in a just God, a man who cannot bring himself either to deny that God exists, or to deny that He is just, such a man is led perforce to seek God with all his soul. And one can see how well suited such an anxious search of God is to nourish and to strengthen personal religion.

It is already much, in the first place, to keep trust in God in the dark night. The design of God is not easy to grasp.

"That which Zeus hath set his heart upon is not easy to track out. Surely everywhere, even in darkness, it bursts into flame with dark destiny before the eyes of human folk. . . . For shaggy and thick-shaded stretch the paths of his devices, which none may perceive nor explore."[37]

"Zeus, whoever he be—if to be called and invoked by this name is pleasing to him, even thus do I address him. I have nothing whereto to liken him, weighing all in the balance, nothing save Zeus, if there is need to cast the burden of vain thought from the care-laden mind in real truth."[38]

"Thou who supportest Earth and of whom Earth is the support, Zeus, whoe'er Thou art, hard to surmise and to know, Nature's inflexible Law or Mind dwelling in mortal men, to Thee I lift my praise; for, noiseless as Thou walkest, Thou leadest according to justice all that happens here below."[39]

If God is just, if God is wise, and if the ways of God lead of necessity to a good end, we have only to understand these ways.

The solution given by the tragic poets is that suffering teaches man and makes him better. "It is Zeus who has put men on the way to wisdom by establishing as a valid law, 'By suffering they shall win understanding.' "[40]

When the chorus of the *Agamemnon* proclaims this famous axiom, it is of course thinking primarily of the Grecian king. However terrible may have been the dilemma in which he was caught, yet Agamemnon did commit a wrong in sacrificing his daughter Iphigenia. From that moment, he must suffer.

But the formula has a more profound meaning as well. Life is after all rarely so simple as to present us a man entirely innocent or entirely guilty. Let us take the example of Agamemnon. "A heavy doom indeed is disobedience"—disobedience to the order of Artemis to kill Iphigenia,—"but a heavy doom too if I rend my child, the delight of my house."[41] Meanwhile the army is waiting, drawn up on the shore of Aulis, waiting to sail and dying of hunger. Plague is setting in, and all the other difficulties attendant upon the delaying of a campaigning host. It is for Agamemnon, and for him alone, to put an end to this delay. He has but to sacrifice Iphigenia, and the anger of Artemis will straightway be appeased; a favorable wind will blow, and they can weigh anchor and set off. In truth, what ought a general to do in such an extremity, what *can* he do? But Clytemnestra will not be consoled for the death of her daughter. When the Chief returns, she will kill him. And one day, the son will come back from a foreign land to avenge his father. That is the plot of the *Oresteia*. We witness a whole succession of murders. And each time we ask ourselves the question: "Is this a crime? Is it not rather one of those tragic situations in which, whatever we do, disaster is sure to fall upon us? Or again, as in Clytemnestra's case, is not the motive one of those deep impulses of flesh and blood which nothing can resist?" Even so, in Homer, did Agamemnon excuse himself for the taking of Briseis from Achilles: "It is not *I* who did it, but *Zeus*, and Fate, and, walking in darkness, Erinys."[42] Aeschylus corrects this too simple view: "Fate was a *partner* to this death, my child."[43]

Thus men are more or less led on by obscure forces which they neither see (Erinys comes unseen)[44] nor understand, and which, almost in spite of themselves, cause them to err. Undoubtedly, man is not entirely free of responsibility. Our faults are not altogether due to "Blindness, daughter of Zeus."[45] But fate is really a partner. Now one begins to understand the role of suffering. "Surely there is a blessing from the gods, who, using force, sit on the dread bench of the helmsman."[46] By suffering, we learn to see the ways of God. Patroclus' death leads Achilles to abandon his wrath. And later, when old Priam comes to ask for the body of Hector, Achilles, having himself known suffering, receives the unhappy father like a brother in universal human sorrow.

Suffering, then, teaches. At the least, it teaches pity. Heracles slowly awakens from the death-sleep which followed his delirium. Theseus, king of Athens, whom he had rescued in days gone by, bends over him. And Theseus says to him: "I am not afraid to share misfortune with *you*, / For I had joy once."[47] In the past, Theseus had a son. He too, in a moment of blind folly, brought about this son's death. He is able to understand Heracles. He pities him. He manifests the second benefit of suffering; that it ennobles. "The noble man endures / All pitfalls from the gods and does not shrink."[48] And so, little by little, Heracles, who wanted to kill himself, accepts life. Suicide is easy: to continue to live is finer. "I will be strong to await death."[49] Heracles obeys because it would be cowardly to die. "Must I, quitting life, prove me craven?"[50] Thus he has an obscure awareness that there is something worth more than life itself, more even than happiness; it is to be faithful to the ideal that one has set oneself, to the most godlike part of oneself. Which is the same as to say: to be faithful to God, and to God's plan. And thus we find here, as you can see, a presentiment of union with the Will of God. "And now I must obey Destiny," says Heracles.[51] And the Stoic Cleanthes will say, for his part: "Lead me, O God, and thou my Destiny / To that one place which you will have me fill. / I follow gladly."[52]

⬦   ⬦   ⬦

I should like to end these observations on the Quest of God in the Classical Age with a portrait of one of the most remarkable religious personalities of the fifth century, Heraclitus of Ephesus. Heraclitus can, besides, be regarded as the forerunner *par excellence* of Plato. Like Plato, he is an aristocrat who, disgusted with the bad government of his fatherland, withdraws far from the world to meditate upon eternal things.

He was descended from King Codrus, the founder of Ephesus. The title of "king" and the sacerdotal function attached to it were hereditary in his family. But although his rank, therefore, assured him of a role in the affairs of the city, the beginning of the fifth century was the time, in Ionia as in Megara and in

Attica, when the old aristocracy had to make way for the representatives of the newer classes, shipowners, merchants, and industrialists. And the hatred of superiority that is characteristic of democratic rule was as strong in Ephesus as elsewhere. After the exile of his friend Hermodorus, "the most capable man in the city" (fr. 121),[53] Heraclitus withdrew to the sanctuary of Artemis. There he was said to play at knuckle-bones with children—an occupation which, he said, was better than to take part in politics with such colleagues. Plato was to speak in the same vein. If we are to believe the legend, even this retreat was not enough. Heraclitus sought deeper seclusion in the mountains near Ephesus. There he lived as a hermit, feeding on herbs and wild fruits. There too, as the legend has it, he died, at the age of sixty.

This legend must undoubtedly contain some elements of truth. The little that remains of Heraclitus' writings does in fact suggest a proud personality, who, confident that he has seen the essence of things, regards the human comedy as a child's game (fr. 70).

Strife prevails everywhere (fr. 53). But this disorder leads to an Order. For the struggle itself, the incessant change from one state to its opposite, produces in the end a Harmony (frr. 8, 51, 54). This Harmony lies in the fact that everything in the universe obeys a certain measure, or *metron*. The cosmic fire flames up and dies down "with measure" (fr. 30). The passage of the elements into one another, fire into water into earth, and then earth into water into fire, is balanced in both directions (frr. 31, 60). In short, there is an eternal Plan governing all this, a Plan which is a Logos, a Logos which is Zeus. And by Zeus must be understood God himself, the ruler of the universe.

God and his Justice. You will recall the importance of the role of Justice in Hesiod's poem. In the *Works and Days*, however, the Justice of Zeus was applied only to men. Fish, wild beasts, and the birds of the air devour one another; for them, no justice (*W.D.* 277 ff.). If Hesiod recounted the fable of the falcon and the nightingale (202 ff.), it was only to contrast the brutal society of the animals with that of men, which should be governed by Justice (213 ff.). But a little later, Archilochus corrects the Hesiodic fable by that of the eagle and the fox.[54] Hesiod's nightingale had no recourse against the might of the hawk; Archilochus' fox, threatened by the eagle, turns to Zeus and says: "O Zeus, Father Zeus, Thine is the rule of Heaven. Thou overseest the deeds of men, alike knavish and lawful. But Thou takest count also of the rightdoing or wrongdoing of beasts."[55] Thus Zeus keeps watch over the animal world as well, and we may wonder if Archilochus had not already some intuition that the incessant change of Nature is a regulated movement, a *rhythmos*.[56] This last advance is certainly apparent in the statement of Heraclitus (fr. 94): "The Sun shall not transgress his limits. Else will the Erinyes, the servants of Dike, be on his trail." Here Justice passes from the moral to the cosmic plane. Zeus is the final Reason who moves and who explains the universe.[57]

But this Reason is hidden. The true Harmony is not apparent (fr. 54). Because men live their life as if they were asleep (fr. 1), being at once present and absent (fr. 34), the supreme Reality escapes them. He who is truly wise "seeks himself" (fr. 101) in solitary contemplation; that is, he seeks within himself the key to the puzzle of things. In so doing he discovers that all is one (frr. 10, 41, 50); that all, in the eyes of God, is resolved into beauty and order (fr. 102), and that this unity of the Whole is the purpose (γνώμη) of God who through all things governs all things (fr. 41).

In a word, then, the wise man finds peace and rest in God. Another Ionian, Archilochus, in the extremity of human suffering, found no other remedy than the endurance (τλημοσύνη) of a stout heart standing firm against destiny.[58] This fair courage remains the special mark of Greek wisdom. In the fourth century of our era, Sallustius, the friend of Julian, still says that the virtue of fortitude is sufficient for happiness.[59] But he adds that the souls who live in accordance with this virtue are united to the gods and share with them the rule of the universe. They have knowledge of the plan of God and they adhere to this plan. This is precisely the goal which Greek philosophy set itself from the fifth century onward. One may say that, of those who lived before Plato, Heraclitus of Ephesus, who may have been the inventor of the word *philosophos*, most clearly showed the path to this goal.

III

The Hellenistic Mood
and the Influence of Plato

WE HAVE seen thus far in certain Greeks of the
Classical Age two forms of personal religion, that is, of personal
union with the divine. There is a more concrete form, whereby
man communicates in tender and loving intimacy with one or
another of the Olympians. And there is a more inward form,
whereby man in the presence of human misery and of the enigma
of the will of God desires to leave this world for that of the gods,
or seeks to penetrate God's plan, or resigns himself to accept
this plan as that of a wise and just God.

We must now attempt to determine how these attitudes of
the soul were influenced, first, by the conquests of Alexander
and his successors, the conquests which open what historians
call the Hellenistic Age, and secondly, by the teaching of Plato.

As to the first point, we must, by way of caution, make one
observation. In general, where there is no direct evidence, it is
always difficult to measure the influence of political changes on
the religious dispositions of individuals. Of their influence on
the exterior and social aspect of religion there can be no doubt.
Thus at the time of Alexander's conquests the two major political facts—first, the loss of autonomy in the Greek cities, and,
second, the contact and then the mingling of Greeks and Orien-
tals—clearly had their repercussions on religion. On the one
hand, the protecting deities of the Greek cities lost in importance. This is an undeniable fact; even if the outer form of the
cult, as for example in conservative Athens, did not change, yet
it is perfectly clear that the feeling of the public toward Athena
was quite different in the fifth century, when Athena was the
symbol of the Athenian empire, when the gold reserve of the

37

state was deposited in the Parthenon under the protection of
Athena, and the Hellenotamiae offered to the goddess, as "first-
fruits" (*aparche*), one-sixtieth of the tribute paid by the subject
allies.[1] Clearly, men's feelings toward the goddess at that time
were not the same as in the year 304, when Demetrius Poliorcetes established himself as a living god in the Parthenon as the
brother of Athena.[2]

Moreover, the new contacts between Greece and the lands of
the East introduce into Greece new cults and prepare the way
for the fusion which is commonly called syncretism. But how
does this affect intimate feelings? How, in particular, does it
affect the personal piety of the humble Arcadian shepherd, of
the laborer, of the seaman? And how does it affect piety in
the home? Why, and in what way, should great political events
have had any echo in the hearts of all those good folk who, un-
disturbed in their homely labors, went on working the fields as
before?

This applies especially to the first form of personal religion,
that symbolized in the pair Hippolytus-Artemis. But there is
another observation which concerns more closely the second
form. In the sphere of religious feeling, the influence of a spiritual hero—of a philosopher among the ancients, or of a saint
in Christianity—may carry far more weight than any political
circumstance. I will give a very clear example from the history
of Christian piety. You know how the representation of Jesus
changes in the course of centuries, and with it the very attitude
of the Christian toward Our Lord. The Byzantines knew him
best as Christ Pantocrator, the Lord of the Universe, who is
represented in the mosaics decorating the cupolas and apses of
so many churches of Greece, Sicily, and Italy. In a direct line
from the Pantocrator, in the High Middle Ages, comes the
Christ in Majesty who adorns the tympanum over the main
portal of the Romanesque church. Then there comes, in the
fourteenth century, and continues from that time, the Christ in
Passion, the bleeding Christ, nailed to the cross and bending his
head, often represented in the most realistic manner. One might

think, and quite naturally, that the Christ in Passion has some immediate relation with the terrible miseries of the fourteenth century: the unending wars between the Italian cities, the Hundred Years' War in France, and especially the Black Death which devastated the West. These events may have effected some change, but they are not essential to an explanation. The true cause was the personality of a saint, St. Francis of Assisi, and his personal devotion to the suffering humanity of Jesus.

With all due reservation, I believe that the spiritual hero Socrates and his interpreter Plato—under whatever light one may regard this interpretation—had an equally great influence on the ages which followed them, at least for the second form of personal religion, which is more inward and more intellectual than the first.

The theme of this chapter, then, is twofold.

First, I should like to devote a paragraph to showing how certain conditions of life in the Hellenistic and Greco-Roman ages were such as dispose men's souls to union with the divine.

My second point, and the essential one of this chapter, is to show how Plato dominated in part the spirituality of the following ages in its most inward and intellectual form.

I

Now, to show what were the conditions of life which promoted personal religion in the Hellenistic Age would be an enormous task. And, as many have already studied the matter, I may restrict myself to three short observations.

First, we must note a tendency to prefer the hidden life, the life in retreat, which Plato had already, in the famous passage of the *Republic* (VI 496B-E), recommended to the wise man when the affairs of his country have become too corrupt,[3] the life which Aristotle had exalted in his *Protrepticus*, and of which Epicurus becomes the exponent and the living example in his garden. This love of withdrawal in the great Hellenistic and Imperial Roman cities becomes a current of such strength that it merits a study of its own. Such will be the subject of my next

Love of withdrawl

chapter. Be it noted here that it naturally predisposes man to the contemplative life, to union with the divine. As Plato showed in the *Phaedo*, there can be no *theoria*, no contemplation, unless a man has composed himself in peace. This becomes a fundamental principle of all mystic doctrine.

Secondly, because, perhaps, of a certain diffidence toward the old civic gods, we see that the Hellenistic Man betakes himself, if he is of a religious temperament, to one of the many groups formed around the chapel of a new divinity, of a divinity, namely, either entirely new or, if it is Greek, yet now appearing in a new form. One enters a *thiasos*, an *eranos*, a *koinon*. The name may vary; the essential characteristics are the same. The groups of the Old World, the tribe and the brotherhood, were both civic and religious and a man became a member of them on a hereditary basis. There was no choice involved; it was all decided in advance. But now, in these new groups, there was a choice. A man could choose a group honoring one divinity in preference to a group honoring another. He could choose, for example, Isis, or the Syrian Aphrodite, or Cybele with her Attis, or even the God of the Jews, or again Dionysus, whose cult was now widespread in all the Hellenic East, or Asclepius, the healing god, the god of consolation. One can see right away how significant such a choice would be for religious psychology. The god to whom a man entrusts himself is his god by choice; and the very fact of his choice is proof of a personal religion, which can lead to a more intimate bond than would otherwise exist between the chosen god and his worshiper.

One more important feature of the Hellenistic Age was favorable to personal union with a god: the sense of the instability of human affairs. Here political circumstances play a decisive part. No more tormented period of world history is to be found than the first centuries of the Hellenistic Age. There were countless wars among the successors of Alexander, and countless changes of fortune. Today's victor was tomorrow's vanquished; think only of the career of Demetrius Poliorcetes. Among the kings of Macedonia, of Syria, of Egypt, war was unending. The

Greek cities were now the ally of one power, now of another. Then rises the power of Rome, and a series of Roman conflicts with the Achaean League, with Philip V and Perseus, with Antiochus III. In the wake of all these wars comes misery. The fields are laid waste; the sea is infested with pirates; a secure life is nowhere to be had. The type of the hardened soldier, the mercenary, becomes common. With all this is born and finds widespread acceptance the notion that everything in this world is governed by a cruel and inconstant power, by Tyche or Fortune, or even by Chance (τὸ αὐτόματον), a power entirely indifferent to the individual man, who is like a frail craft tossed about on the rough waters of life. This idea of Fortune, applied at first to public affairs,⁴ is transferred to private. How can any man believe in a just and wise Providence? The life of every one of us is directed by the blind goddess. These ideas find their way into the novel. The *Metamorphoses* of Apuleius give us an example.

Or again, under the influence of the astrological doctrines which, from the third century on, at least in Egypt, became popular, men believed that all things are ruled by an inexorable fatality (in Greek: Heimarmene) which from the moment of our birth determines the entire course of our lives, and which nothing can enable us to escape. In opposition, then, to Fortune or to Heimarmene, certain gods appear as Saviors. Asclepius, for example, saves not only the sick. We shall see by the example of Aristides that he can be regarded as a spiritual guide in all the difficulties of existence. Isis does more than save men from the perils of the sea, and invent all the arts on which human society is based. In her aretalogies, the accounts of her powers, she is said to be greater than Heimarmene: Fatality must obey her; hence she has the power to deliver men from its grip.⁵ Isis and Serapis on the one hand, and Asclepius on the other, work miracles for their devotees. We have accounts of such miracles in the Hellenistic Age and later, and there is no reason to doubt that from then on the cults of Isis and of Asclepius gave rise to feelings of personal piety similar to those that we shall see later in the Lucius of Apuleius and in the rhetorician Aristides.

II

Let us go on to Plato. This is naturally not the place to remind you of the Platonic philosophy. I take a knowledge of it for granted. My purpose is to show what aspects of that philosophy have influenced decisively the spirituality of later ages. Besides, in a great philosophic doctrine, that which exercises the most profound influence on men's souls is neither always nor even mainly that doctrine's logical and metaphysical structure. The influence comes rather from the ferment which gives the whole doctrine its life; from the impulse that leads it in one particular direction, from the impulse that lies in the heart of the philosopher and communicates itself to our hearts.

What, then, is the profound current which moves the Platonic doctrine? It is an impulse toward the Eternal.[6] Only the Eternal exists, because it alone is unchanging. All else, all that the senses perceive, is fleeting and corruptible. They pass, the Eternal remains.

What is the Eternal, which does not pass?

It is of course the *noeton*, the intelligible, that is, the essence of a thing, of a man, of a dog, or what not, susceptible of definition (*logos*) and of being named (*onoma*). It is that essence because, while concrete objects come into being, change continually, and perish, the essence is unchanging. Yet when one reads Plato one soon sees that it is not the essence of concrete objects that interested him. It is not the essence of concrete objects that he gives as example in the *Phaedo*, the dialogue in which the metaphysics of the Ideas appears for the first time; it is rather the Just in itself, the Equitable in itself. The essence of concrete things is, as it were, forced upon him by the logic of the system, and even brings him into much difficulty, as one can see from the well-known problems of the *Parmenides*. They are not the primary object of his search. The primary object is what we today should call the supreme categories of Being: the Beautiful (the *Symposium*), the Good (the *Republic*), the One (the *Philebus*).

essence

primary object

And how do we apprehend this primary object? There must be a complete purification of the subject: detachment from the world, the contemplative mood, the turning of the soul upon itself. You will remember the teachings of the *Phaedo* and especially the famous image by which the soul is presented to us as an octopus shrinking into itself, the celebrated passage which made of the *Phaedo* the spiritual guide of antiquity.

Then there must be a purification of the object (the *Symposium*, the *Republic*). In the example given in the *Symposium*, one begins with the contemplation of a beautiful boy, and from there one passes to a twofold abstraction. First one goes from the beauty of *one* boy to the beauty of *all* boys; then one goes from the beauty of boys, who are still, after all, concrete objects, to the beauty of less material things, of the sciences and arts, of actions and occupations.

This stage once arrived at, it is no longer a question of an abstraction, but of a leap into the unknown—what Diotima, the priestess of Mantinea, calls the great mysteries: *the perfect initiation*. Up to this point the object was *noeton* in the true sense of the word; it was an object which could be understood, the essence of which could be entirely mastered. Now, one must advance to the Beautiful in itself, an object admitting neither of definition nor of name. The *Symposium* is positive on this point, and the text, in my opinion, leaves no room for doubt.[7]

Observe that, in Plato, essence (*ousia*), definition (*logos*), and denomination (*onoma*) go together and are interchangeable:[8] to say *ousia* is to say *logos*, to say *logos* is to say *ousia*. But the Ocean of the Beautiful to which we finally come in the *Symposium* is above *onoma* and above *logos*. Thence it is no more an *ousia*, it is above *ousia*. From this we can see that neither is it *noeton*, an intelligible thing, in the true sense of the word. It is given this name because it is clearly of the order of the intelligible, and therefore other than the sensible (*aistheton*). But in reality it is superintelligible. It is apprehended by the *nous*, the mind, qua faculty of mystical cognition. I say "mystical," the proper term, because, in the last degree, one no longer understands. There is merely a touching (ἐφαπτομένῳ *Symp.* 212A 5), the touching of which the mystics speak to designate the ineffable contact by which they attain the supreme object.

That this is indeed the meaning of the *Symposium*, and that this doctrine of the *Symposium* results from a personal and intimate experience of Plato himself, is proved by two texts, one from the *Republic*, and the other from the *VIIth Letter*.

To say *logos*, let us repeat, is to say *ousia*, and in the *Symposium* we were attaining an object above *logos*. Now, in both the *VIIth Letter* and the *Republic*, at the final step of the ascent to the Good, we attain an object which is above *ousia*: "The Good itself," says the *Republic*, "is not essence, but transcends essence in dignity and power." (*Rep.* VI 509B 8 ff.).

Let us read, on the other hand, what is said in the *VIIth Letter*, where Plato describes the cognition of the supreme object: "There is no writing of mine on this subject, nor will there ever be; for it cannot be put into words like other objects of knowledge: you spend much time together, you live together in the pursuit of this thing; and then, suddenly, like a flame kindled from a leaping fire, it comes into your soul and feeds itself" (341C 4–D 2).

I am for my part convinced that this is the expression of a personal experience. In sum, the supreme object of knowledge, the final degree of our metaphysical investigations, the term on which all the rest depends, is an object which defies definition, and hence cannot be named. It is the Unknown God.

Now this doctrine, as we shall see, was to have an incalculable effect upon pagan mysticism from the second century of our era onwards. The doctrine of the Undefinable God (ἀόριστος) or of the Ineffable God (ἀκατονόμαστος) was to be current among the second-century Platonists—in Numenius, in the Chaldaic Oracles, in the Hermetic Writings. Here God is no longer the subject of a rational, but of a suprarational, knowledge, a knowledge to be attained only in silence, when one has stilled not only every sensation and every passion, but also every reflection, every movement of discursive thought (διάνοια).

This leads us to a matter of the greatest importance for the understanding of Platonic mysticism, both in Plato and in his successors. I mean the ambiguous pair of words *noeton* and *nous*. We translate them, in English, by "intelligible" and "intellect" for want of anything better. But these translations are inadequate, and it might be better to transcribe the Greek words as they are. The *noeton* is certainly the intelligible in the true sense of the word, the object that we can comprehend and define. But at the same time it is the object above the intelligible, the object we can neither comprehend nor define, which we attain only by mystical contact. In this last case, by terming the object *noeton*, we only define it negatively, opposing it to the *aistheton*; we do not define it positively. We can only say: it is an ocean of joy in which we submerge ourselves, it is a beyond, an above, an *epekeina*. The same ambiguity exists for *nous*. Certainly it is the faculty of intellection. But it is also the faculty of mystical contact. Sometimes it is translated "spirit," to distinguish it precisely, in this latter function, from the intellective faculty; but spirit, which properly translates *pneuma*, "breath," belongs to a tradition quite different from the Platonic. It is best, as I say, to transcribe the words *noeton* and *nous* and keep in mind their double meaning.

◇ ◇ ◇

Thus Plato stands at the beginning of the great mystical tradition which, through Plotinus and Proclus, inspired Pseudo-Dionysius, John Scotus Erigena, and which then, through the latter or even directly—I am alluding to the medieval translation of certain treatises of Proclus—exercised so great an influence in the Middle Ages, notably on the mystical writer from the Rhineland, Meister Eckhart, and on Nicholas of Cusa. I say nothing of modern instances.

But Plato stands also at the beginning of another spiritual tradition which was no less important in antiquity, and which was especially so throughout the Hellenistic and Greco-Roman periods, until the second century of our era, when there was a return to the Platonic metaphysical doctrine of the Ideas.

The first tradition, which we were describing a moment ago, we can call the desire of union with the ineffable God.

The second, which we are now about to consider, we can call the desire of union with the God of the world, the cosmic God.

I should like to show first how Plato came to give his attention to the world and to make of contemplation of the world the supreme object of wisdom; and, second, how that contemplation of the world became, until the last days of antiquity, the spiritual and moral fare *par excellence* of educated pagans.

Plato, at the time when he was elaborating the metaphysics of Ideas, seems to have taken no interest in the phenomena of the sensible world. These phenomena were by definition excluded from investigation, being essentially changeable, whereas the object of knowledge must be unchangeable. Even in the *Republic*, when Socrates outlines the educational program of the future philosopher-legislator, Glaucon's proposal that the science of the stars (astronomy) be placed on this program draws a protest from Socrates. The visible stars are still concrete things. It is true that they present to our eyes a beautiful celestial embroidery; yet they are not objects of knowledge (*Rep.* VII 529AB).

However, there is in Plato more than one man. There is the metaphysical geometer. There is the man athirst for the Eternal. And there is also the reformer. It is the reformer who will lead to the scientist, to the *physikos*, the natural scientist as antiquity knew him, that is, as "he who seeks to understand the nature of things, *Physis*."

The *Republic* had sketched the portrait of the ideal city. Yet Plato was aware that the city is made up of living men, men who are not pure intelligence, but made of flesh and blood, endowed with a material body with its own passions and set in a material world which acts upon them and to which they react at every moment. This being so, the most idealistic reformer, if he wishes to exert a real effect and not content himself with dealing in the abstract, must face the problem of the human body and of its environment, and therefore of matter, of the structure of matter, and of the laws which govern it. Thus it is that we pass from the *Republic* to the *Timaeus* by an almost inevitable logic. The philosopher-legislator cannot afford to neglect knowledge of the sensible world.

But herein lies the difficulty. Can the world be known? According to the principle heretofore guiding every step of Plato's philosophy, the sensible, as such, is unknowable, since it is changing. How, then, does one find the unchanging in the Cosmos? The answer is that if there is nothing absolutely unchanging in the Cosmos, there is nevertheless something relatively unchanging. The stars do change, for they are continually in movement. But this movement is recurrent and presents an order. The heaven of the fixed stars travels every day in the same path about the earth (such, with the one exception of Aristarchus, was the notion of all antiquity). As for the planets, they may at first appear to be wandering stars, but reflection shows that their movements obey regular laws and are susceptible of calculation. It was precisely during the lifetime of Plato that Eudoxus and Callippus determined by calculation the laws of planetary movement. From this it appears that there is order in the heavens, and this order, which cannot be attributed to chance, necessarily manifests an intelligence.

Whence comes this intelligible movement of the heavens? All autonomous movement comes from a soul. Plato proved this in the *Phaedrus*, and he repeats the proof in the tenth book of the *Laws*.[9] All regular movement implies not only the motive action of soul simply because there is movement, but, since it is a regular movement, the action of an intelligent soul. One thus comes finally to the notion of an intelligent World-Soul, a notion which henceforward dominated ancient thought.

Let us go on to man. Man, too, is composed of a body and a soul. But whereas, in the heavens, the relations between body and soul are normal ones, the two component parts being well adjusted to each other, so that the composite organism is moved in a regular pattern, in man, on the contrary, body and soul are ill adjusted. The body is made of gross matter, obedient to blind necessities. When the soul, coming from heaven, related to the stars and made of the same stuff as they are, falls into the material body, the resulting organism is moved in a disordered manner; one has only to see the chaotic agitation of a newborn child's legs and arms. Hence one must educate the movements of man, from the first movements of the child to the entire behavior of the adult. And since the soul comes from Heaven, since it is of like nature with the stars, and since the stars present an eternally regular movement, wisdom must consist in putting the movement of man in accord with those of the stars. That is the conclusion of the *Timaeus*, one of the noblest passages of Plato.[10]

These, it seems to me, were the intellectual steps by which Plato was led to his doctrine of the world. He has not repudiated the theory of the Ideas; he mentions this theory again in the *Timaeus*, and the great metaphysical dialogues of the *Parmenides* and the *Sophist*, in which he reëxamines, criticizes, and corrects this theory, are contemporary with the *Timaeus*. He has lost nothing; he has only gained. His ever-alert curiosity has enabled him to assimilate the latest discoveries of his friend Eudoxus and of his disciple Callippus. His thought, constantly in motion, has perceived how these discoveries allow us to solve the mystery of man and to integrate man into the universe. This enrichment of Platonic doctrine was to have the most important consequences both for theology proper and for personal religion.

Let us first take theology. Plato, like many of his contemporaries, was aware of the decline of the Olympian deities. He was likewise aware that the young men of Athens were undergoing a grave spiritual and moral crisis. The complaints of the young man in the *Laws* (book X) must be taken seriously. He no longer believes in the traditional gods. Nor does he believe in Providence. But the State, as the ancients conceived it, cannot do without religion. The ancient state is not "secular." This leads Plato to reconsider the whole problem of God and to construct what can well be named the first philosophical theology.

The Unknown God, this Ocean, this ineffable abyss which we approach at the end of the ascent of the *Symposium* and of the *Republic,* cannot be a civic God, that is, the universally recognized object of the common worship of the city. He is a Hidden God. The knowledge that can be acquired of him by a sort of supernatural contact demands a long interior preparation of which few men are capable. And even the rare person who is able to approach him must do so in the privacy and quiet of his monastic cell, as an individual apart from the city. Finally, such a god cannot be represented. No image of him can be offered to the commonwealth, no image to whom the city as a unit can give prayer and sacrifice. What, then, will become of religion, of that religion which is the foundation of the city? Hence a double task is urgently imposed upon the governing philosopher. He must restore the idea of God and the idea of divine Providence. He must bring to the city as a whole and to the individual new divine objects. The tenth book of the *Laws* answers the first need. The answer to the second is found in the *Epinomis,* which, for my part, in agreement with A. E. Taylor and others,[11] I am willing to consider a genuine unfinished work of Plato.

God exists, but there is no longer any question of the Olympians. Plato does not suppress them. Indeed, he suppresses nothing that was part of the religion of his forebears. But in the *Timaeus,* as in the *Laws* (and the *Epinomis*), he speaks of them with disdain. God exists, and he is the Soul of the Cosmos. This intelligence which eternally moves the world and whose perfect wisdom is manifested in the very order of cosmic movements must of necessity be a divine intelligence. On the other hand, the Cosmos itself, his body, is divine. So in their turn the stars are gods and quite visible ones, which can be worshiped by the city in common and by the citizen in private. The demonstration of the existence of God (I omit here all its details) having once been established, it is an easy matter to prove that this God is provident. What is it that keeps the young man in the *Laws* from believing in Providence? It is the apparent disorder of human things. Crime not only goes unpunished, but triumphs. The good man is wretched. To what end, then, the practice of virtue? If God takes no interest in our lives, there is every reason to make use of pure force, to practice the morality of "might makes right" upheld by Callicles in the *Gorgias*. Let us hear Plato's answer: "Let us persuade the young man by our discourse that all things are ordered by him who cares for the world with a view to the preservation and excellence of the whole, whereof each part, so far as it can, does and receives what is proper to it. To each of these parts, down to the smallest fraction, rulers . . . are appointed to bring about fulfillment even to the uttermost fraction; whereof thy portion also, O perverse man, is one, and tends therefore in its striving toward the All, tiny though it be. But thou failest to perceive that all partial generation is for the sake of the whole, in order that for the life of the world blissful existence may be secured. For it is not brought into being for thy sake, but thou art for its sake."[12] Memorable words, which will echo far into the ages to come. "Each portion," says Plato, "looks to, and tends ever toward, the All," εἰς τὸ πᾶν συντείνει βλέπον ἀεί (903c 1). And Marcus Aurelius (XII): "Let your impulse be ever to look to the All," εἰς τὸ πᾶν ἀεὶ ὁρᾶν. And again Plotinus (II 9, 9.75): "Look always not for what is pleasant to you, but for the good of the All."[13]

The idea of God and Providence once restored, there remains the task of founding the new religion, that of the Cosmic God or of the astral gods. I have previously attempted to show how the new religion put forward in the *Epinomis* is meant by the author to be a public religion, destined to replace in the city the outworn cult of the Olympians.[14] The attempt of the *Epinomis* was, in fact, not a success. The worship of the stars did not become official till much later, and for brief periods only—under Aurelian in the third century, and under Julian in the fourth. And the cult of the sun promulgated by these two emperors was, besides, permeated with Oriental influence, quite foreign to anything in Plato.

On the other hand, the religion of the Cosmic God, or of the Cosmos as a god, or even of the stars, was the current form of personal religion among the majority of educated pagans, from Cleanthes in the third century before Christ to Simplicius in the fifth century of our era. The silent contemplation of the Cosmos nourished and fortified many noble souls. It even led to the sort of union with God which Cumont, in a famous article, named "astral mysticism." I shall devote a chapter to this spiritual movement. Here, in conclusion, I should like to show how the two forms of Platonic religious philosophy fit in with deep currents in the Greek soul.

We laid it down, in our last chapter, that the sense of the contrast between the happiness of the gods and the miserable state of man had given rise, in the Greek soul, to two traditions. The first was the desire to escape. Ah! to leave this earth, to fly to heaven, to be like unto the gods and partake of their bliss! This was the idea of φυγή, of flight, and of ὁμοίωσις θεῷ, becoming like god. This idea is predominant in Plato from the *Phaedo* to the *Theaetetus*. It is not absent from the *Timaeus*: to set the motion of one's soul in accord with the motion of the heavenly bodies, to lose oneself in the contemplation of the stars, is to forget for an instant the frailty and the fleetingness of the things of the earth, to immerse oneself in the Eternal.

The second tradition was the passionate search for God, and we have seen on this point that Zeus assumes two aspects. In one aspect, he is the just God, the guarantor of eternal justice:

> It was not Zeus, I think, made this decree,
> Nor Justice, dweller with the gods below,
> Who made appointment of such laws to man.
> Nor did I think your edicts were so strong
> That any mortal man might override
> The gods' unwritten and unmoving laws.
> Their life is not today and yesterday,
> But always, and none knoweth whence they came.
>
> (Soph. *Ant.* 450 ff.)[15]

I am for my part firmly persuaded that the Eternal Laws of
Zeus, which never change, but stand unshakable in the aether,
are the prototypes of the supreme Ideas of Plato, of the eternal
worlds of the Good, the Beautiful, and the True, which the
souls contemplated in the heavens before their fall to earth. If
so, we have discovered a direct line from one of the noblest
beliefs of the fifth century to that doctrine which is Plato's
chief glory.

In another aspect, Zeus is a hidden God, whose ways are
impenetrable or at best difficult to comprehend, so that union
with God becomes a union with the divine Will, a submission
in faith to God's plan. We have already seen the assertion of this
noble theme at the end of Euripides' *Heracles*. It is the same
theme that finds expression in the conclusion of the *Timaeus* and
in Plato's answer to the young man in the *Laws*. What does it
mean, after all, to set oneself in accord with God, if not to
accept what God wills? And how can one accept this, if it is
not that one has persuaded oneself that what God wills is wise
and good, since it is God who wills it? that in the end it must
serve the cause of the good? that this final Order, which I do
not see, which remains hidden from me, is the true order of
things, being, as it is, the plan of God? I shall show what weight
these ideas had for Stoic morality, and how, through the Stoics,
they nourished all pagan wisdom. I shall also show how, in
Cleanthes, in Marcus Aurelius, they assume a specifically religious form. May I content myself here with pointing out that
this doctrine of resignation[15] found its first philosophic expression in Plato, and that even before Plato it answered to a courage and nobility innate in the Greek soul, in that Greek soul—
let us remember this—which forged the ideal of the hero.

IV

The Inclination
to Retirement

IT IS a well-known fact among all the theorists of
the spiritual life that you cannot find God unless you retire from
the crowd and collect yourself in solitude and peace of mind.
Examples of this may be seen in the next four chapters. Lucius,
the hero of Apuleius' novel, retires into the temple of Isis and
communes all day with the image of his beloved goddess. Aristides retires into the sanctuary of Asclepius at Pergamum to
think only of the revelations of his God. Marcus Aurelius says
(IV 3, 1): "Men seek retreats for themselves in the country, at
the seashores, on the hills, and you yourself are always yearning
after such places." And we read in the *Hermetica* (X 9): "Who
is the man," asks the disciple, "who has knowledge and is divine?" And Hermes answers: "He is the man who speaks not
many words nor listens to much talk. He who spends his time in
disputations and in listening to men's words is beating the air,
my son; for knowledge of God the Father cannot be taught by
speech nor learnt by hearing."

To introduce our subject of personal religion in the Hellenistic and Greco-Roman world, it seems, then, useful to watch
the progress of this notion of retirement. There is in Greek a
specific word for it. "To retire" is *anachorein.* "To retire into
oneself" is *anachorein eis heauton.* The man who has retired from
the world is the anchorite. We shall observe the evolution of
these words from the second century B.C. onward. The changes
in their meaning will allow us to see the changes of mood in
those who used them. First, then, let us take *anachorein* as an
absolute.

53

"Anachorein": To Retire

Perhaps the best examples of this use are to be found in reference to the man of politics. We find many such examples in Polybius, though here the word does not yet imply that total detachment from the world which will be its meaning in later times.[2] A politician, that is, may find it expedient to retreat without, for all that, making a final renunciation of politics. Polybius' case was, it seems, of this sort. In 29.10.5 it is said that Polybius himself and his group (οἱ περὶ Πολύβιον), in order not to oppose the order of a Roman legate, withdrew from state affairs (ἀνεχώρησαν ἐκ τῶν πραγμάτων). Similarly in 28.3.4 the Roman envoys traveling through the Peloponnese announce in each city that they know the names of those who thus withdrew contrary to their duty (τοὺς ... παρὰ τὸ δέον ἀναχωροῦντας) as well as the names of those who have embraced the Roman cause (τοὺς προσπίπτοντας). The antithesis reveals the situation clearly; those who withdrew from office wished to avoid trouble for themselves. Even more clear is 30.10.5; having defeated Perseus, the Romans are completely triumphant in Greece, and they have not one outspoken opponent, "for all those who were against the Roman party *yielded to circumstances and entirely withdrew* (διὰ τὸ τοὺς ἀντιπολιτευομένους ἅπαντας, εἴκοντας τοῖς καιροῖς, ἀνακεχωρηκέναι τελέως). The passage 28.3.8 is decisive: there is a rumor that C. Popilius had in the Achaean assembly accused Lycortas, Archon, and Polybius "of having abandoned the Roman party to live for the time being in retirement (καὶ τὴν ἡσυχίαν ἄγοντας κατὰ τὸ παρόν), *not because they were naturally inclined to the quiet life* (οὐ φύσει τοιούτους ὄντας), *but because they wanted to keep an eye on events and await the propitious moment*" (ἀλλὰ παρατηροῦντας τὰ συμβαίνοντα καὶ τοῖς καιροῖς ἐφεδρεύοντας).

Anachorein in this absolute sense seems to have been current ·by the time of Cicero, who, writing in March of the year 48, to Atticus (IX 4), tells him how, in order that he might be out of the fray and yet continue to concern himself with political problems (*ut et abducam animum ab querelis et in eo ipso de quo agitur exercear*), he has examined a number of political propositions (θέσεις πολιτικαί) on the attitude to be assumed by the statesman living under a tyranny.

Among these θέσεις we find this in IX 4, 2: "Can a good citizen, living under a tyranny, withdraw and live in idleness?" (εἰ πολιτικὸν τὸ ἡσυχάζειν ἀναχωρήσαντά ποι, τῆς πατρίδος τυραννουμένης). This text is very instructive. For a Roman of the Republic that would be an abnormal, almost culpable, choice; he would not make it unless he were constrained to do so. Some years later, when Augustus is *imperator*, the exception becomes the rule. We can understand, then, how under the emperors of the first century the tendency toward ἀναχώρησις could spread among the Roman nobles.

The same reasons may also explain how the Epicurean sect came to have so many adherents. For that very withdrawal far from worldly commerce was a dogma of their school.[3] We have a charming and a little-known text bearing on that very point; I should like to bring it to your attention.

In his treatise περὶ οἰκονομίας[4] Philodemus asks what the attitude of the wise man should be toward the πορισμός, that is, toward the means of providing oneself with the necessities of life. To obtain them through warfare he finds blameworthy: "to maintain that the best method of getting sustenance for oneself is to live by the sword . . . is typical of those who thirst for fame but are devoid of either of the two wisdoms,[5] as could clearly be seen from the very lives of those who write of such things. In a word, they think apparently that the only successful life is that led by statesmen and by men of action, so much so that they ask frequently what possible advantage a man can find in dedicating himself to truth and to leisurely consideration of everything of this [abstract] kind. For, to their mind at least, with regard to the good things which contribute to the tranquillity [happiness] resulting from the noblest causes, these men are not at the same time men of action and contemplatives, but, they will say, it is clear that these great specialists in truth either do not possess the virtue which brings about that end [happiness], or else do not draw from the truth any accomplishment worthy of esteem, or that the proof of their eminent wisdom will be made when they have a city to govern or forces to lead."[6] To derive one's means from the breeding of horses is ridiculous, from the exploitation of mines by servile labor unenviable, from those two sources by working oneself, pure madness. Miserable also is the lot of the farmer who works with his own hands. "But," says he, "to live off the land while others farm it—that is truly in keeping with wisdom. For then one is least entangled in business, the source of so many annoyances; there indeed is found a becoming way of life, a withdrawal into leisure with one's friends, and, for those who moderate their desires, the most honorable source of revenue" (καὶ διαγωγὴν ἐπιπρεπῆ καὶ μετὰ φίλων ἀναχώρησιν εὔσχολον καὶ παρὰ τοῖς [σώφροσι]ν εὐσχημονεστάτην πρόσοδον).[7]

We have just seen the position of the Epicurean. It is interesting to make a comparison of it with that of the Stoic. A text of Musonius comes to our aid. He asks himself (fr. 11, pp. 57 ff. Hense)[8] exactly the same question as Philodemus: What source of income best becomes the wise man? (τίς ὁ φιλοσόφῳ προσήκων πόρος;) After having named one or several which Stobaeus does not mention,[9] he goes on to the working of the land as a source of profit (πόρος ἀπὸ γῆς). He then allows himself to speculate on how no life is so well adapted to philosophy as the shepherd's. The cultivation of the soil, painful for the body, risks tiring the soul as well, but the shepherd's calling does not prevent the soul from meditating upon some great subject and thus becoming wiser (p. 58, lines 19 ff., Hense: τὴν ψυχὴν ἐκλογίζεσθαί τι τῶν κρειττόνων κἀκ τῶν τοιούτων λογισμῶν αὐτὴν αὐτῆς γίνεσθαι σοφωτέραν.) Therefore, he says, it is the shepherd's life that I approve most highly. Nevertheless the farmer's calling has its advantages too, for it is the most natural and the most healthy, and if one is capable of doing the two things at once, cultivating both the soil and philosophy, no other walk in life could be compared to it. "But I ask you," Musonius, who cannot forget his role as a teacher of wisdom, hastens to remark, "is it not strange that the teacher, a man capable of leading youth into philosophy, should till the soil and labor with his body like a peasant?" "Yes, if the tilling of the soil should prevent him from pursuing philosophy and from helping others to advance in wisdom. But, in fact, young men seem to me to progress more rapidly, not when they gather around a teacher in the city and limit themselves to listening to him while he lectures (p. 60, line 11: ἐν τῇ διατριβῇ), but when they see him cultivating the earth and practicing what he preaches, namely, that it is better to toil and to endure fatigue than to beg one's living from another" (p. 60, lines 13–15 Hense: καὶ ἔργῳ ἐκδεικνύμενον ἅπερ ὑφηγεῖται ὁ λόγος, ὅτι χρὴ πονεῖν καὶ κακοπαθεῖν τῷ σώματι μᾶλλον ἢ ἑτέρου δεῖσθαι τοῦ τρέφοντος). A remarkable conclusion, which illustrates to perfection the difference between the two minds. The fact remains, however, that nostalgia for the rural life is evident alike in Musonius and in Philodemus.

This use of ἀναχωρεῖν, ἀναχώρησις, taken absolutely in the sense of "retreat far from the world," leads in a straight line to the spiritual meaning which the word will have under the Empire. The example of Cicero is a case in point, and one has only to open one's eyes to see instances in any period: the man of action is no sooner torn from his manifold occupations than, if he has in him the stuff of a philosopher, he is led to ask himself the more serious questions which concern all mankind. The withdrawal from the world (ἀναχώρησις) leads in turn to the withdrawal into oneself (ἀναχωρεῖν εἰς ἑαυτόν). But before entering on this second aspect it might be well to exclude another absolute meaning of ἀναχώρησις, which, although it may perhaps offer certain superficial analogies with Christian anchoritism such as we find in Egypt from the third century on, yet exerted no influence whatever on the spiritual "retreat" of the pagans of the West.

This other use of ἀναχωρεῖν is in fact peculiar to Egypt; it has reference to economic conditions in that country under the domination of the Ptolemies and of Rome. It often happened that the peasants, crushed by taxes and tolls, left their village to withdraw (ἀναχωρεῖν, ἐκχωρεῖν) either to a place of asylum or to some village where they might be hidden, or even to swamps or the desert (ἀναχωρεῖν εἰς τὴν ξένην, εἰς τὴν ἐρημίαν), where they led the life of outlaws. These flights, which could be isolated or collective, constituted a kind of strike, which the government tolerated while it did not sanction it as a right.[10] Now it is quite probable that among the peasants who became anchorites and buried themselves in the desert in imitation of St. Anthony, there must have been some of those unfortunate, oppressed souls, or others who were fleeing the world from some less noble motive. And it is also possible that the use of the word ἀναχω-ρητής for the hermits of Egypt was influenced by that local usage.[11] But that is no more than a fortuitous conflux of tradi-tions, which does not at all explain the origin of Christian monasticism and has not the least resemblance to the ἀναχωρεῖν of a Seneca or a Marcus Aurelius.

"Anachorein eis heauton": To Retire into Oneself

To my knowledge, the expression ἀναχωρεῖν εἰς ἑαυτόν first ap-pears in the authors of the Roman Empire, where it is possibly a development from the then current usage of ἀναχωρεῖν alone to mean "go into retirement." A near equivalent, however, is found long before this, and we ought not to be surprised that it is in the writings of the master of Hellenistic spirituality, Plato. Plato himself depends on Socrates, and it may be said that the example of Socrates gave the movement its initial impulse.[12]

Everyone knows the significant passage from the *Symposium* (175AB). Socrates has been invited to dine at the house of Agathon and is making his way thither in company with Aristo-demus. All at once, "turning his attention inward upon him-self,"[13] he lags behind and lets Aristodemus go on ahead. The latter arrives at Agathon's, believing that the philosopher is following close behind him. But soon there comes a slave who announces (*loc. cit. supra*): "Socrates has gone off to one side and is standing in a neighbor's doorway, and will not come in when

I call him" (Σωκράτης οὗτος ἀναχωρήσας ἐν τῷ τῶν γειτόνων προθύρῳ ἔστηκεν, κἀμοῦ καλοῦντος οὐκ ἐθέλει εἰσιέναι). Then when Agathon tells the slave to insist, "Let him alone," Aristodemus interrupts; "it is a sort of habit he has. From time to time he draws apart from us wherever he may be and stands there. So don't bother him." (ἐᾶτε αὐτόν. ἔθος γάρ τι τουτ' ἔχει· ἐνίοτε ἀποστὰς ὅποι ἂν τύχῃ ἔστηκεν, 175Β 1–3.)

There can be no doubt that this living example of Socrates influenced the doctrine attributed to him by his disciple in the *Phaedo* concerning concentration (67c 7, 83A 6). Purification consists in separating as much as possible the soul from the body; the soul must learn to isolate itself, to draw itself together as a mollusk retracts and detaches itself at all points from its shell (67c 6, αὐτὴν καθ' αὑτὴν πανταχόθεν ἐκ τοῦ σώματος συναγείρεσθαί τε καὶ ἀθροίζεσθαι: also 83A, 7, αὐτὴν εἰς αὑτὴν ξυλλέγεσθαι καὶ ἀθροίζεσθαι), and thus to retire from all sense impressions (83A 6, ἐκ τούτων [sc. τῶν αἰσθήσεων] ἀναχωρεῖν), living alone with itself (67c 8, οἰκεῖν . . . μόνην καθ' αὑτήν, and 64c 7, αὐτὴν καθ' αὑτὴν εἶναι). Here we have, it seems, not only the idea of concentration, but also the origin of the later phrases ἀναχωρεῖν εἰς ἑαυτόν and μόνος πρὸς μόνον, "to retreat into oneself," and "alone with the Alone."

This enables us to understand those texts of authors of the Imperial Age wherein, political ἀναχωρεῖν and spiritual ἀναχώρησις having become one, retiring from the world is joined to retiring into oneself; and so important does this last become that these moralists declare it avails nothing to abandon the city unless one has learned to collect one's soul, and that in case of necessity the wise man will find it sufficient to concentrate in the midst of the crowd.

The Idea of Concentration Under the Empire

Let us begin with the most famous work, Seneca's *Epistulae Morales ad Lucilium*. One outstanding thought in these letters is that one must shun the crowd. "You ask me what, above all else, we must avoid? The crowd." Thus *turbam* in 7.1, with which compare 8.1 and *NQ* IV praef. 3: *a turba . . . te separa*; also in *EM* 10.1: "avoid the many, avoid the few, avoid even one man" (*fuge multitudinem, fuge paucitatem, fuge etiam unum*). "Hide yourself in leisure (*in otio*), but hide your leisure too." However, it is no good to run hither and yon in search of solitude; that is only more agitation. "I am coming to have a good opinion of your future; you do not run about nor do you distract yourself by perpetually changing your abode. For such restlessness reveals a disordered spirit. The first sign, to my thinking, of a well-ordered mind is the ability to remain in one place and pass the time in one's own company" (*consistere et secum morari*: *EM* 2.1). *EM* 28.1: "It's your soul you must change, not your environment" (*animum debes mutare, non caelum*). *EM* 55.8: "Where one lives means little for one's peace of soul; it is the mind that must render all things agreeable to itself." *EM* 69.1: "Your continual movings, your unending scurryings about, do not please me . . . such changes of residence show an unstable soul. The soul cannot through retirement grow into unity until it has given over its casting about and its roaming."

It is as if one were hearing the advice of a modern doctor to a neurotic patient. Now the second idea has come to complete the first. To withdraw is in vain if one does not withdraw into oneself. It can be done even in society. *EM* 25.6–7: "I shall gradually enable you to follow the precept of Epicurus: the best moment of all to enter into yourself (*in te ipse secede*) is when you are forced to be in the midst of a crowd. . . . Yes, provided that you are a good, tranquil, and restrained man; otherwise, you had better take refuge with the crowd and away from yourself (*in turbam tibi a te recedendum est*); for going into yourself you are keeping company with a scoundrel." Clearly spiritual retreat (ἀναχωρεῖν, *secedere*) is like a touchstone; to be capable of it is to have a heart already pure and detached, so that truly to enjoy this retreat far from the world one must begin by purifying oneself. When this is accomplished, any place is good for contemplation. Seneca himself, if we are to believe him, learned to maintain tranquillity in turmoil. *EM* 56.1: "May I instantly perish if it is true, as they say, that silence is indispensable for one wishing to confine himself to study. All around me I hear only diverse cries; I am surrounded by noise." The poor fellow has been forced to take lodgings above a bath house, in which are practiced not only bathing and massaging, but every kind of gymnastics as well, weight lifting, the throwing and catching of balls in some game in which the counting aloud by the scorer is a feature in itself, and also discussion, argumentation, quarrels, to say nothing of the barber, the vendors of wood and of food, each of whom makes himself known by his special cry. Seneca has hardened himself against all these miseries; "for I force my mind to concentrate upon itself (56.5: *sibi intentum esse*; cf. the ἑαυτῷ προσέχειν τὸν νοῦν of *Symposium* 174D 5) and keep it from wandering to outside things. All outdoors may be bedlam so long as there is no disturbance within. . . . For of what good is a completely quiet neighborhood (*totius regionis silentium*) if our emotions are in tumult?"

That Dio Chrysostom dedicated one of his Λόγοι (*Discourses*) to the ἀναχώρησις[14] proves that the subject and the discussion of it were then much in fashion. Here we find Seneca's two principal themes again. On the one hand, silence and withdrawal are favorable to meditation. "The cultivation of the mind (παιδεία) and philosophy, which best leads to that end, require, it seems, solitude and retirement in full measure (πολλῆς ἐρημίας τε καὶ ἀναχωρήσεως τυγχάνουσι δεόμεναι); and just as the sick, unless they are surrounded with peace and silence, cannot find sleep,[15] so with students of literature (τοῖς φιλολόγοις); unless they have complete silence when they are working, if any object distracts their view, if any sound comes to their ear, their soul cannot direct its attention to its affairs [thought], nor can it apply itself wholeheartedly."[16] Nevertheless, on the other hand, one can do without external silence, and it is useless to journey from one land to another in quest of calm. "It is not the man who travels from city to city, from locality to locality, who can be said to be making his retreat (ἀναχωρεῖν), for wherever he goes, there will arise difficulties enough to keep him from having time to do what he ought." Dio's conclusion is that of Seneca: "it may well be that the best and most profitable retreat is the retreat into oneself (ἡ εἰς ἑαυτὸν ἀναχώρησις, Seneca's *ad te recedere*) and the concentration upon oneself (προσέχειν τοῖς αὐτοῦ πράγμασι), whether one is in Babylon, or in Athens, in camp, or alone on a small island.[17] For retreats and voyages of this sort (ἀναχωρήσεις καὶ ἀποδημίαι) do little for the leisure of the soul, nor do they help one to do what one ought (πράττειν τὰ δέοντα)."

"Even in camp" (ἐάν τ' ἐν στρατοπέδῳ) "peace can be found." Such was the saying of Dio. For Marcus Aurelius, who so many times found himself obliged to command armies, this saying had perforce to hold true. A physical withdrawal he would have welcomed. "Men seek for themselves retreats," he writes in his *Meditations* (IV 3, 1), "country houses,[18] places of refuge by the seashore or in the mountains. And you too have a longing for such things." But alas! the emperor, bound to his duties, cannot allow himself such leisure. Hence he continues (IV 3, 2): "All this reveals great naïveté since one possesses the possibility, whenever one wants to use it, of retiring into oneself (εἰς ἑαυτὸν ἀναχωρεῖν). Nowhere is there a withdrawal more calm, more free from care, than into one's own soul. . . . (3) Therefore make this withdrawal constantly, do not cease to become a new man. . . . (9) In short, be mindful of that withdrawal which you can make in the spot of earth where you now are."[19]

The appearance of this tendency to retreat in Seneca, in Dio Chrysostom, in Marcus Aurelius, ought not to lead us to conclude that it is a feature of Stoic ethics. On the contrary, Lucilius attributes to Seneca the statement that Stoic morality definitely obliges one to live in action until one's dying day. *EM* 8.1 reveals Lucilius saying, a little scornfully perhaps: "You order me to shun the crowd, to withdraw myself (*secedere*), and to be content with knowledge of myself (*conscientia esse contentum*)! Where are your fine precepts in virtue of which a man must die in activity?" Seneca answers that by hiding himself he makes himself more useful to others. But it is a weak answer. The truth is that Seneca's motive is not obedience to the dogmas of a school, but a desire inevitably born of an old and weary civilization, especially a metropolitan one. In proof of this, note that we find the same inclination in the Platonic contemplative, Philo, living in Alexandria,[20] while we do not find it in the Stoic Epictetus, a man of different temperament, who likes the life of the city.[21] The contrast is significant. For Philo ἐρημία, solitude, is a great blessing, the indispensable condition of any profound thought. When we wish to yield ourselves to profound meditation on any subject, we take refuge in the desert (εἰς ἐρημίαν ἀποδιδράσκομεν), we close our eyes, stop up our ears, bid our five senses farewell (*Legum Allegoria*, II 25).[22] Philo, of course, like Seneca and Dio, does not forget that, properly to enjoy solitude, the heart must be void of passions. "Many a time I have forsaken kinsfolk, friends, and home, and buried myself in the wilderness (εἰς ἐρημίαν ἐλθών) to give my attention to some subject worthy of contemplation,[23] only to derive therefrom no profit, but to have my spirit, bitter and distraught by passion, wander to matters of a contrary kind. But then again, at other times, I have been in the midst of a great throng and have had a collected mind (ἠρεμῶ τὴν διάνοιαν). God has dispersed the crowd that besets the soul and has taught me that favorable and unfavorable conditions are not brought about by differences of place, but by God, who moves and leads the chariot of the soul in whatever way he pleases." (*Leg. Alleg.* II 85.) But the desert is nonetheless propitious to union with God; the Essenes and the Therapeutae gave witness of this. To Epictetus, on the contrary, the word ἐρημία means an evil; for him this word means not solitude but desolation.[24] "Desolation is the state of that man who is without help (κατάστασίς τις τοῦ ἀβοηθήτου). For a man can be alone (μόνος) but not *forlorn* (ἔρημος), and he can be forlorn in the midst of his fellows" (III 13.1). "When we have lost a brother, or a son, or a friend whose life we shared, we call ourselves abandoned and forlorn, notwithstanding that we may be in Rome, with great crowds on all sides of us, with a large company in our house, perchance with a multitude of slaves of our own" (III 13.2).

It is not only the interior desolation that one feels, but the lack of support from without; ἔρημος, for Epictetus has only the primitive meaning of the word when accompanied by a genitive, "empty"—of something. The ἔρημος is the man who is without aid and thus a prey to whoever wishes to harm him, for example, the traveler who falls into the hands of brigands. "For it is not the sight of a human being as such that puts an end to our forlorn state, but of one who is faithful and decent and willing to help" (III 13.13).[25] Thus solitude may be termed an evil. "For we have within us a natural instinct which leads us to live in society, to love one another, to take pleasure in commerce with one another" (III 13.5).[26] "Nonetheless one must prepare oneself for this too (to be alone), that is, one must be able to be sufficient unto oneself and to live in the company of oneself" (δύνασθαι αὐτὸν ἑαυτῷ ἀρκεῖν, δύνασθαι αὐτὸν ἑαυτῷ συνεῖναι). Zeus, who lives alone, devotes his thought unceasingly to the government of the universe; just in the same way, the consolation of the wise man will be to contemplate the world-order and to remedy, so far as he is able, the evils in the state of man. (III 13.8.) This is the true Stoic doctrine; it can be seen how far removed it is from the ἀναχώρησις. The latter is, in truth, more the case with the contemplative, with the man who concentrates upon his soul and upon study, with a Philo, or a Seneca, or a Marcus Aurelius.[27] Plotinus confirms this.

Plotinus uses ἀναχωρεῖν or ἀναχώρησις at least twice in the sense of "inner retreat." In I 1.12, 18 we read: "There is then another life, other activities [sc. than those of the composite body and soul], and that which is chastised [sc. the composite] is other [sc. than the soul itself]: the soul retires and separates itself (ἡ δὲ ἀναχώρησις καὶ ὁ χωρισμός) not alone from the earthly body, but from everything that is attached to itself." II 3.4, 14 ff.: "Thus must we flee from this world (cf. *Theaet.* 176A) and separate ourselves from all that has been added to us; thus must we cease to be this composite thing, this animate body, slave to the corporeal nature which has barely preserved a trace of the soul; all that depends on this life is corporeal. It is to that other soul, the soul that comes from without, that the movement upward belongs, the movement toward beauty, toward the divine which is the slave to no thing. Either one makes use of this other soul in order to be a transcendent object and to live the life of a transcendent object, *being retired into oneself* (κατὰ τοῦτο ζῆν ἀναχωρήσας), or else one is deprived of the soul and lives in the bonds of Fatality; then the stars are no longer only signs for us; rather we become ourselves like a fragment, depending on the Whole, of which we are a fragment." Plotinus besides had himself a love of withdrawal. From time to time he would take refuge in Campania in the estate of his friend Zethus (Porphyrius, *Vit. Plot.* 22: ἐχρῆτο δὲ αὐτῷ οἰκείως, ὡς καὶ εἰς τοὺς ἀγροὺς πρὸς αὐτὸν ἀναχωρεῖν); it was there that he died (*ibid.* 2.17 ff.). And of course we know Plotinus' beautiful dream. This was the time of the romantic *Lives* of the philosopher Pythagoras which depicted in idyllic colors the life of his disciples in rural monasteries. We have already seen how Musonius recommended the use of his διδασκαλεῖα, his philosophic homilies, in the country. Plotinus wanted to make this dream a reality. With him were associated not only his pupils and his friends, but also many young boys and girls entrusted to him by their parents before their death in order that they might be assured a good education (*ibid.* 9). Since he enjoyed the favor of the emperor Gallienus and of the emperor's wife, he asked them to restore for his use a small town in Campania, at that time completely in ruins. It was, so the story goes, to be named Platonopolis, and there the laws of philosophy were to be observed. Plotinus himself engaged to withdraw (ἀναχωρήσειν) there with his companions (*ibid.* 12). The project apparently came to nothing, and it was perhaps just as well. Yet it affords testimony of that nostalgia for quiet which each generation feels anew in that weary society which is cut off from everything because it has exhausted everything,[28] whose only aspiration now is repose: *o beata solitudo, o sola beatitudo.*

THE CHRISTIAN USE OF "ANACHORESIS"

Now we are come to the Christian ἀναχωρητής, to the anchorite. I have already mentioned the claim that the terms ἀναχωρεῖν, ἀναχώρησις, ἀναχωρητής in monastic literature derive from the Egyptian usage of the words to cover the cases of peasants taking refuge from taxes and tolls. On *Pap. Lille No. 3*, where the perfect tense ἀνακεχώρηκε meaning "has fled" ("er ist geflohen") is found, Ulrich Wilcken writes: "Dass man später die Christen, die sich gerade hier in Ägypten zuerst aus der Welt in die Wüste zurückzogen, ἀναχωρηταί genannt hat, ist kein Zufall."[29] ("It is no mere coincidence that those Christians who precisely here in Egypt for the first time have withdrawn from the world into the desert should have been called ἀναχωρηταί.") I, on the contrary, am of the opinion that it is just a case of pure chance, or at least that if the Christians bethought themselves at all of the local usage of the word, it was only owing to an exterior resemblance which had little or no influence on the profound sense with which they endowed it. This becomes evident, to begin with, when one studies such learned writers as Origen and Athanasius, especially the contemplative Origen. He has not only the normal usage of ἀναχωρεῖν to designate spiritual withdrawal—the word comes naturally to his pen, for he knows his pagan authors,—but he has also the accent of personal experience, of that same aspiration which so deeply concerns his compatriot and contemporary Plotinus. Or how else can we judge the following exquisite passage: "It is most of all when one knows oneself to be miserable and suffering, the object of hate on account of what one says and teaches, it is most of all then that one repeats 'I withdraw myself. What have I to do with this turmoil? If even my teaching, if the publication of my lessons is only to cause me pain, would it not be far better to take refuge in peace and solitude?' (διὰ τί οὐχὶ μᾶλλον ἀναχωρῶ ἐπὶ τὴν ἐρημίαν καὶ ἡσυχίαν ;)."[30] Or again, speaking of Luke 1:80 (which tells how John the Baptist lived in the desert: " 'And the child was in the deserts' says the Evangelist. . . . So he did not stay with his father and mother, but withdrew (ἀνεχώρησεν), fleeing the tumult of the city, the cruelties of the mob, to take refuge in solitude and give himself to prayer (ἵνα ἐν ταῖς ἐρημίαις τυγχάνων . . . εὐχαῖς σχολάζῃ)."[31] And when Athanasius writes in his life of St. Anthony (*Vit. Anton.* 45): "Meanwhile, withdrawing by himself (καθ' ἑαυτὸν ἀναχωρῶν), as was his wont, to his hermitage (μοναστήριον), he continued to live in austerity. Each day he groaned at the thought of the mansions of heaven and aspired to have a place in them whenever he contemplated the impermanence of our human life,"[32] he expressed himself just as Porphyry would have done concerning his master Plotinus. But what of Palladius? And what of all the popular tales of the lives of the Egyptian monks? In the works of these uncultivated men, at least, does not ἀναχωρεῖν derive from the local, popular usage? Has not the "flight" of the Christian anchorites been compared to that of the Egyptian fellahin? Here again the relation, if it exists at all, seems to me superficial. By that time ἀναχωρεῖν was almost a technical term for "withdrawal from the world." And if these popular biographers had not read the pagan philosophers, at any rate they knew Athanasius' *Life of St. Anthony*, which was then one of the most popular religious writings among the monks. Most of all, they knew the gospels where they could read: "When Jesus heard of it, he departed thence . . . into a desert place apart" (Matt. 14: 13: ἀνεχώρησεν . . . εἰς ἔρημον τόπον κατ' ἰδίαν), or "he departed again into a mountain himself alone" (John 6: 15: ἀνεχώρησεν πάλιν εἰς τὸ ὄρος αὐτὸς μόνος). And they knew further that for forty days the Spirit of God had led Jesus into the wilderness, there to live in fasting and prayer and spiritual combat. This was the example, effective above all others, which brought about the "flight" of the Fathers to the desert and gave to their gesture its full meaning.

Role of Fortune
Semi-autobiographic

contemplation
Glory life in
Vocation
Mystic
Love

V

Popular Piety

Lucius and Isis

You remember the subject of the *Metamorphoses* of Apuleius. Lucius, a young man of noble family,[1] rich, cultivated, and well brought up, is making a business trip on horseback, attended by a few slaves, and arrives at Hypata in Thessaly, a country renowned for its magicians. It so happens that Lucius is extremely curious about magic; and, as he is staying at Hypata in the home of a friend of his father's, whose wife, Pamphile, knows all the formulae of the magical arts, he cannot rest until he has found out their secrets. He insinuates himself into the good graces of the young maidservant of Pamphile, and through her obtains a drug which, if he anoints his body with it, will transform him into a bird—the desire to fly is one of the oldest ambitions of humanity,—while another drug will thereafter restore him to human form. But the young servant, Photis, confuses the boxes, and, instead of being transformed into a bird, poor Lucius is changed into that hideous, lascivious, and ridiculous animal despised by antiquity—an ass (I–III).[2]

Then begins for the ass Lucius a series of unfortunate misadventures. He falls into the hands of brigands, who, after a while, determine to kill him, together with a beautiful girl whom they have carried off (IV–VI): it is to charm this girl that the horrible old woman who keeps house for the brigands tells the story of Psyche (IV, 28–VI, 24).

Delivered from the brigands along with the young captive, by the latter's husband, Lucius believes himself to be called to a less arduous life, when Fortune delivers him over to new woes (VII). He is bought in turn by priests of the Syrian Goddess

68

(VIII–IX), a miller, a market gardener (IX), and then passes
into the hands of a soldier. He is finally sold by the soldier to
two slaves, a cook and a baker, and now eats royally; for
although his shape is that of an ass, his tastes nonetheless remain human. The two slaves catch him one day in the act of
feasting upon meat and cakes prepared for human consump-
tion, and, instead of becoming angry, burst out laughing. The
master of these slaves hears about Lucius, and, delighted with
such a find, begins to exhibit in town after town this extraordinary ass that behaves like a human being. All goes well until,
having reached Corinth, the master wishes to display Lucius
the ass in the act of intercourse with a woman sentenced to be
thrown to the wild beasts. This proposal revolts Lucius, and
he flees to Cenchreae, a Corinthian port on the Saronic Gulf.

That brings us to the story of our hero's deliverance (XI,
init.). Lucius arrives in the evening and finds a secluded beach
near the port of Cenchreae on which to rest. Overcome by
weariness, he falls asleep. Meanwhile night has fallen, the sea
is calm, everything is peaceful. Suddenly Lucius awakes, and
sees the full orb of the moon rising from the sea. Then, moved
by the solemnity of the hour and the beauty of the scene, knowing that the moon is an all-powerful deity,[3] aware that Destiny
is at last offering him the hope of deliverance by placing him in
the presence of this goddess, he arises, purifies himself by plung-
ing his head seven times (a sacred number) into the waves, and
addresses a touching prayer to the moon, in which he voices his
distress.[4] He invokes the Queen of Heaven under various names:
Ceres, Venus, Diana, Proserpina, Hecate—for he does not know
which suits her best, and it is always a good idea to give a god
his real name,—and in his prayer he implores the goddess to
bring to an end his trials and adventures, and to restore him to
his former shape. If that be impossible, then may he at least be
allowed to die (XI, 1–2).

Thereupon he once more lapses into slumber, and sees appearing before him, coming out of the sea, not one of the goddesses
he had named, but Isis.[5] For Isis, in the time of Apuleius, is a

powerful goddess who governs the whole universe, and unites in herself the qualities and attributes of all the goddesses, and who, under an infinitude of names, is adored as one and the same deity in every country.[6]

Isis comforts Lucius. Henceforth she takes him under her protection; he has therefore nothing more to fear. The next day, which is the feast of the *navigium Isidis*, celebrated on March 5, there is to be a solemn procession from the city to the beach. Coming last in the procession, the priest of the goddess will be holding a wreath of roses. Let Lucius eat it and, from an ass, he will change back into a man. After this miracle, Lucius will have to devote his life to the goddess: "and if, by acts of careful obedience, pious service, and steadfast self-discipline,[7] thou comest to deserve my favor, thou shalt know that I, and I alone, have the power to extend thy life beyond the bounds appointed by thy fate" (XI, 6, 7).

The next day comes, and everything happens as the goddess has foretold. The procession files past (XI, 7–11).[8] Bringing up the rear comes the priest who, himself warned in a dream, offers the wreath of roses to the ass, who devours it. Immediately Lucius resumes his own shape (XI, 12–13). He is clothed (XI, 14);[9] and the priest, as through prophetic ecstasy,[10] describes for him the new life he is going to lead (XI, 15);[11] the people congratulate him (XI, 16); and he himself joins the procession and takes part in the festivities until they reach the temple of Isis at Cenchreae. There, as he cannot be separated from the goddess, he rents lodgings within the sanctuary enclosure, shares, as a layman, the life of her priests, and spends long hours every day in contemplation of the statue of Isis.[12] Moreover, almost every night, Isis appears to him in dreams and exhorts him to be initiated as her servant (XI, 19, 2). Yet he still hesitates, held back by religious awe, frightened by the austerities of the new life (XI, 19, 3). One day, however, after a dream (XI, 20), he makes up his mind and goes in search of the high priest (*primarium sacerdotem* XI, 21, 2). But this time it is the latter who declines. No one can be initiated unless Isis herself has fixed the day, chosen the candidate, and indicated the cost of the ceremony. The initiation is indeed a formidable act, a kind of voluntary death followed by the vouchsafing of a restoration to life;[13] it would be an offense bringing death (*noxa letalis*) to accomplish this act without having been called. Meanwhile Lucius should prepare himself by rigorous abstinence from impure and evil foods (XI, 21, 7–8). The greatly longed-for hour comes at last. Isis makes known her will; the initiation takes place (XI, 22–24). Lucius, in the height of joy, remains a few days more in the temple. Then, after having addressed a fervent prayer to Isis (XI, 25) and tenderly embraced the priest, he returns to his native land (XI, 25, 7).

He does not stay there long, for a few days after his arrival Isis sends him to Rome. There he leads the same life as at Cenchreae, praying without ceasing at the temple of Isis on the Campus Martius,[14] when, a year having passed (XI, 26, 4), he is told in a nocturnal dream that he must now be initiated into the mysteries of Osiris (XI, 26, 4–28, 6).[15] He submits, although his purse has been greatly depleted by the cost of the first initiation, the trip to Rome, and by the cost of living in the capital, which is greater than in the provinces (XI, 28, 7). Finally, in yet another dream, Lucius receives the order to undergo a third initiation. A little astonished at first by these costly favors of the divinity, Lucius nevertheless obeys. He is rewarded by Osiris, who predicts for him a fine career as a lawyer,[16] and has him enter the college of pastophori (XI, 29–30). So ends the novel.

There exists on the XIth book of the *Metamorphoses* an abundant literature,[17] and it may therefore seem that little remains to be said about that part of the work. But the books and articles bearing upon it are concerned either in a general way with the cult of Isis or more particularly with the passage on the mysteries (XI, 22–24). My plan is different, and in a sense, new. Everything has doubtless been said on the mysteries of Isis. Every approach has been attempted; comparison with the Eleusinian Mysteries and hypothesis of a kind of mystical drama acted out before Lucius (Lafaye, Cumont);[18] explanation by a state of trance and by magical devices (de Jong);[19] explanation by the ancient Egyptian religion and by doctrines related to the Cosmic Elements (Reitzenstein).[20] All that, however, is only conjectural,[21] and we should be wasting our time if we tried to discover what Apuleius wanted to keep secret. What concerns us here is something else, namely, Lucius' sentiments toward Isis, his religious attitude. From this point of view we shall ask ourselves, first, what is the meaning of the XIth book in relation to the novel as a whole. Then we shall consider two themes directly related with our subject, union with God: the vocation of Lucius, and his contemplative adoration of the goddess.

THE AUTOBIOGRAPHICAL VALUE OF BOOK XI

First let us ask ourselves what relationship book XI has to the rest of the *Metamorphoses*.

There are two ways of looking at Apuleius' novel. One may see in it simply an amusing story—the model for which was furnished by a Greek novel (the *Ass* of Lucian offers a parallel) —to which Apuleius would then have added an edifying conclusion having no direct connection with what precedes.[22] Or one may suppose that, from the beginning, Apuleius had in mind the events at the end of the work, and may consequently consider the whole novel as a story of a sin and a redemption, a conversion in the proper sense of the word—the passage from a sinner's miserable condition to a pure and sanctified life. For my part I should incline to this second interpretation, for the following reasons. (1) There are in the text itself very clear indications that the role of Isis in the XIth book is conceived in opposition to the role of Fortune or Destiny in the rest of the novel, and that there is therefore a relationship of contrast intended between these two divine powers, with Isis triumphing in the end. (2) It is evident that the misfortunes of Lucius and his moral degradation are actually the consequences of a sin from which he is cleansed and saved by Isis, through whom he comes to lead a new life.

It is a *Leitmotiv* of the novel, especially marked from book VII[23] on, that Lucius is a plaything in the hands of Fortune. Whenever it seems that Lucius' condition is bound to improve, and that he is on the point of reaching a safe harbor, Fortune submerges him once more. Let us choose an example from the VIIth book. In the beginning of this book, after the ass has been rescued from the bandits, his fellow captive Charite, in whose deliverance he was instrumental, in order to show her gratitude, entrusts him to the head groom so that he may graze in leisurely fashion in the fields. However, instead of letting him graze, the groom's wife makes him turn a millstone all day long, striking him whenever he stops. One day he is sent to the fields, but it turns out that the proximity of horses is a martyrdom for the ass. Thus "I was already crushed by these miseries, when relentless Fortune gave me over to new torments" (VII, 16, 1). Next the ass is separated from the horses, and he thinks he is saved. Alas, it is only to fall into the hands of a little slave who does not cease to persecute him; thus "Fortune, that could not have enough of my torments, had devised a new pain for me" (VII, 17, 1). This little slave leads Lucius, the ass, to the mountainside, where he cuts wood and loads it on the animal. One day, however, the ass, frightened by the sight of a bear, takes flight and is caught and mounted by a passer-by. Lucius believes that his trials are over. But he falls into the hands of wicked shepherds, who, to punish him for having abandoned the child, prepare to kill him; "Fortune, ever bent on my distress, put an end with hideous swiftness to my happy escape, and set new snares for me" (VII, 25, 3). Later, put up for sale in a populous and famous city, perhaps Berea in Macedonia, Lucius the ass, wanted by no one, falls into the hands of the lowest of the low— pervert priests of the Syrian Goddess. "But that savage Fortune of mine, from whom I fled through so many lands but could not escape, and whom all the miseries I had undergone did not appease, once more turned her blind eyes upon me" (VIII, 24, 1). While he is in the service of these priests, upon the occasion of their being invited to a banquet in a village by a devotee of Atargatis, Lucius finds himself in deadly peril. At the last moment, a haunch of venison having been eaten by a dog, the cook gets ready to roast and serve the ass Lucius. He flees, and runs headlong into the banquet hall, where he breaks everything. Once more he believes that his misfortunes are at an end: "But assuredly if Fortune is against it, nothing good can come to mortal man; and there is no plan so carefully worked out and no device so clever that it can undo or change in any way the fate previously ordained by the gods" (IX, 1, 5).

Why this cruelty, this relentlessness on the part of Fortune? It is because she is a blind goddess,[24] who is partial only to the wicked and the unworthy, who accords reputation in such contrary wise that the evildoer passes for a good man, and the most innocent for guilty (VII, 2, 5).

Over against malicious Fortune is set, in a striking contrast, the good and merciful Isis. No one can prosper if Fortune is against him, we read in IX, 1, 5, nor can he cancel or amend the fate previously ordained by the gods.[25] No one, that is, except Isis, who by her providence saves men: "Give over thy weeping and leave off thy lamentations; for, by my providence, the day of deliverance already dawns for thee" (XI, 5, 4).[26] "And here at last came the good things which the divinity most present to aid had promised me. The priest came along bearing in his right hand my destiny and deliverance itself in the form of the wreath of roses commanded by the goddess. . . . And fitting it was that it was a crown, . . . for at last I was to be victor over the Fortune that had so cruelly fought against me." (XI, 12, 1.) This contrast between the two goddesses is strikingly brought out by the priest after the miracle of Isis: "Having undergone hardships many and varied, having been driven by the violent storms of Fortune and buffeted about by her highest winds, thou hast come at last, Lucius, to the haven of Rest and the altar of Mercy. Neither thy high birth, nor thy standing, nor again the learning in which thou dost shine, was anywhere of the slightest help to thee. Thou didst fall on the slippery surface of vigorous youth into servile pleasures and didst reap the bitter fruit of an ill-starred curiosity. But nonetheless Fortune in her blindness, by the very enormity of the ordeals to which she subjected thee, succeeded only in bringing thee to thy present religious felicity—so improvident was she in her malice. Let her go now, let her give free rein to her utter fury, let her find another victim on which to exercise her cruelty. Ill luck has no foothold against the lives of those whom the majesty of our goddess has saved to be her servants. The robbers, the wild beasts, thy slavery, thy wanderings back and forth over the roughest roads, thy daily fear of death—of what avail were these to spiteful Fortune? Now thou art safe under the protection of a Fortune, but of one that is not blind; by the splendor with which she shines she gives light even to the other gods. Put on now a more joyful countenance to match the shining raiment thou wearest, join with exultant steps the procession of the goddess who is thy deliverer. Let the godless see, let them see and recognize the error of their ways; behold how Lucius, delivered from his former troubles, now by the providence of mighty Isis doth joyfully triumph over his Fortune." (XI, 15, 1–4.)[27] We have here a living commentary on the last verse of Isis' aretalogy: "I am victorious over Destiny; Destiny obeyeth me."[28]

Another connection, as we said above, between book XI and the other books is that XI concerns a conversion, the passage from a state of impurity to a pure life. This too is stressed by the priest after the miracle: "Thou didst fall . . . into servile pleasures and didst reap the bitter fruit of an ill-starred curiosity" (XI, 15, 1). Two reasons are given for the downfall and degradation of Lucius: first, curiosity about magic, which led him to make his unfortunate experiment at Hypata (II, 1, 1; 6);[29] and secondly, his voluptuous relations with Photis, the young slave of the magician Pamphile. This last is quite unusual in an author of antiquity, for the ancients considered love as a sickness at the worst, never as a real sin. Moreover, the case of Hippolytus shows that, by refusing love, one actually offends a goddess, Aphrodite. We may ask ourselves whether, in the expression "servile pleasures," the accent be not upon "servile"; but the ancients had no prejudices in that respect.[30] Besides, the blunders of Lucius are presented as imprudent rather than sinful. It is by a chain of imprudent actions—his affair with Photis, and the dabblings in magic to which his curiosity impels him, with Photis as accomplice—that Lucius falls into the hands of Fortune, who proves herself relentless. Again, even in the shape of an ass, Lucius preserves the instincts of a sound and honest lad.[31] Nevertheless, it must be admitted that the frivolous tone of books I to X is in contrast with the steadfast self-discipline imposed upon Lucius in book XI.[32]

One may therefore speak, in a sense, of *conversion*. It follows that, as a conversion may not be understood except in relation to the way of life which preceded, there is obviously a connection between book XI and the rest of the novel.

Now all the interpreters of book XI have noted that the tale here takes on an autobiographical character, especially from the time of Lucius' arrival at the temple at Cenchreae. There are at this point accents of warmth and sincerity which are unmistakable; he who speaks thus has been himself initiated, and is recalling his own experience. What is at first only a very strong impression registered on the reader[33] is later confirmed by a slip—perhaps a voluntary slip—in the text itself, in chapter 27. Lucius is at Rome, a year passes, when he is notified in a dream that he must be initiated into the mysteries of Osiris at the hands of a certain pastophorus named Asinius Marcellus. The latter, for his part, has been advised by the god that he must initiate "a citizen of Madaura, truly a very poor man" (XI, 27, 9).[34] This citizen of Madaura is obviously Apuleius himself, who has taken the place of his hero.

It is, then, certainly Apuleius who speaks. Now we know that Apuleius was pious; he speaks in the *Apology* of a statuette of Hermes, to which he addressed his prayers.[35] We know that he was initiated into various mysteries.[36] We also know that he practiced magic; at least he was accused of it, put on trial with that indictment, and it is in vain that he repudiates the accusation, for his defense, which we read in the *Apology*, is scarcely convincing. If we bear all that in mind, the account of book XI of the *Metamorphoses* and the relation of book XI to the rest of the novel take on a much more interesting aspect. It is no longer merely a matter of the artificial joining of a Greek tale—which, as everything leads us to believe, was nothing but a succession of amusing adventures—to an edifying conclusion. The substance of such a tale remains, but Apuleius has changed the spirit. The work, in its entirety, becomes a human document. Lucius was punished for having tried to practice magic. For the same reason Apuleius underwent a very serious prosecution, which might have cost him his life. Like Lucius, he was at that time a young man.[37] Is it absurd to think that the memory of this experience still obsessed him when he wrote the *Metamorphoses*, and that he has there traced for us the story of a soul which fell, which suffered by reason of that fall, and which the merciful hand of Isis raised up and saved?

We now understand the impassioned tenderness which Lucius feels toward Isis. Let us dwell upon two aspects of that tenderness.

Lucius' Vocation

Lucius has been called. In the very first dream-vision on the beach of Cenchreae, Isis tells him so: "Be sure to remember and to keep graven in thy inmost heart that all the remaining course of thy life, even to thy last breath, is pledged to me" (XI, 6, 5).[38] It is only just, adds the goddess; since it is thanks to her that he is resuming his place among men, he must belong entirely to her. This first call is confirmed by the words of the priest after the miracle: "However, that thou mayst be the more safe and the better fortified, enroll thyself in this sacred soldiering to which thou wast not long ago required to give thy oath; dedicate thyself here and now to the service of our religion and take up the voluntary yoke of its ministry. For when thou beginnest to be the slave of the goddess, then thou wilt the more enjoy the fruit of thy freedom."(XI, 15, 5.) Then, once established in the temple, Lucius is summoned anew each night:

"Nor was there even one night or any sleep which was not nourished by a vision and an admonition of the goddess. By the
reiteration of her holy commands[39] she made it known that she
now wanted me to be initiated into her rite, whereto I had long
been destined" (XI, 19, 2). Nevertheless, Lucius still hesitates:
he dreads the austerities of the new life (XI, 19, 3). Then, when
he does make up his mind, the priest refuses, because the final
call has not been given. "He said I should do my utmost to avoid
both recalcitrance and forwardness, neither delaying when I was
called nor being precipitate when I had been given no order"
(XI, 21, 5).[40] At last a definite summons is heard: "In the darkness of night, in words that were not dark, Isis informed me
clearly that the day was come which I had so long wished for"
(XI, 22, 2).[41] The priest, who has also received notice, declares
that the divine orders[42] must be obeyed immediately. Nor does
the helpful counsel of Isis cease after the initiation. It is because
of a *monitus* that Lucius returns home; it is at the order of Isis
that he goes to Rome; and it is as the result of fresh visions that
he is initiated into the mysteries of Osiris (XI, 26, 4–28, 6), and
afterward, for the second time, into those of Isis (XI, 29–30).[43]

We note that this vocation is an honor, a *dignatio*,[44] and quite
an exceptional one for Lucius, who had never formerly been a
devotee of the goddess. Hence it comes that the crowd cries out,
after the miracle (XI, 16, 4): "Happy indeed is he and thrice
blessed. Assuredly it is by the purity and integrity of his former
life that he has deserved such conspicuous heavenly protection;
so much so that he was no sooner somehow reborn[45] than he was
dedicated to the service of the sacred rites." The words "by the
purity of his former life" do not refer to a fact, since the crowd
knows nothing as yet of Lucius' story. They express a hypothesis: ". . . to be thus favored, this stranger must have led a holy
life."[46] Now as we know, this was not the case. And for that
reason the favor granted to Lucius is the more remarkable, and
better exemplifies the goodness of Isis.

Let us examine more closely this theme of vocation. We note,
in the first place, that the summons received by Lucius to be-

come an initiate is not original with Apuleius. Far otherwise
than in the Eleusinian Mysteries, to be initiated into which it
sufficed "to be pure of hands and to speak Greek,"[47] no one was
received by Isis who had not been called by the goddess herself.
Pausanias bears witness to this point.[48] The reason given by
Pausanias is the same as the one we find in Apuleius: these
mysteries are too awesome for the outsider to dare draw near to
them without a formal command, or for the priests to dare to
initiate anyone without a heavenly summons.[49]

Neither is there any originality in the frequency of the nightly
dreams by which Lucius is honored: "Nor was there even one
night or any sleep without a vision and admonition of the goddess" (XI, 19, 2). Aristides in his *Sacred Discourses* tells us that
he too is favored by nightly visions of Asclepius, and has become
so accustomed to them that he can no longer do anything—
purge himself, go to the baths, take a trip—without being
assured by a dream that such is the will of the god. Let us note
that the ancients attributed much more importance to dreams
than we moderns do. To speak only of journeys, we see Lucius
return to his homeland, then travel to Rome, in consequence of
commands received by night. Again, it was after a dream that
St. Paul, having reached the Troad, went from there to Macedonia.[50]

It is possible too that Lucius' hesitation to obey the goddess
after he has been called is but a literary convention. The following theme is, as a matter of fact, quite often found in the tales
of the miracles of Isis, Sarapis, or Asclepius: the god commands
something; the devotee hesitates and puts off obeying because
he finds the task too difficult or too unusual; the god punishes
him for it, and in the end he obeys. A typical example of this
sequence of events is afforded us by a miracle recounted in an
aretalogy of Imuthes-Asclepius (*Pap. Oxyrh.* 1381). Asclepius
orders a man to translate an account of his miracles from
Egyptian into Greek; the man hesitates before this laborious
task, and puts it off from day to day; he falls sick, Asclepius appears to him, and he finally agrees to obey. Aelius Aristides

affords another example. Since he is always sick, or thinks he is, and is always asking Asclepius for remedies, on one occasion the god prescribes a change of diet of which Aristides' friends disapprove. He is assailed by doubts and delays obedience; consequently his malady grows worse.[51] Another factor which might lead one to think that the hesitation of Lucius is likewise a commonplace is that the phenomenon occurs on three separate occasions, after each of the calls to initiation. The first time, Lucius is held back by fear of the rigors implicit in the new life; the second time, by his poverty; and the third, because to his mind two initiations suffice. On the other hand, we may remark that each of these reasons is plausible, and the first is psychologically interesting as well as sound.

The story of Lucius' vocation is not, therefore, entirely original. There is, however, at least one feature which is new. Lucius is not merely called to initiation; he is called to consecrate his entire life to Isis: "Be sure to remember and to keep graven in thy inmost heart that all the remaining course of thy life, even to thy last breath, is pledged to me."[52] It is precisely because the obligation will last as long as life that Lucius hesitates to commit himself; who can be sure of what he will be tomorrow? That is an original touch, practically unknown among the ancients, which can only be compared with religious vocation among Christians.[53]

THE CONTEMPLATION OF THE GODDESS

A second theme of interest is that of the contemplative adoration of the goddess. It is even the most characteristic feature in the devotion of Lucius to Isis. Let us be specific; I say to Isis, because it seems to be for her alone that Lucius reserves that form of adoration. At least the chapters on initiation into the mysteries of Osiris (XI, 26, 4–28, 6) do not contain any analogous indications; Lucius merely says that, once initiated, he observed with full confidence the practices of the kindred worship, and that he drew from it both spiritual consolation and material profit, for Osiris caused him to succeed in his legal cases.

But to Isis he has given his heart. When the procession has reached the temple at Cenchreae after the feast of the *navigium*, the other devotees return home. "But I could not bring myself to move one inch from where I was; looking intently at the image of the goddess I bethought myself of all the adventures I had had" (XI, 17, 5). When the news of the transformation of Lucius had spread abroad, and his slaves, relatives, and friends came to congratulate him, he of course received them, "... but," says he, "as soon as I could, I went again before the face of the goddess . . . , I made my lodgings within the temple precinct, and entirely shared the life of her priests and was an inseparable worshiper of her great godhead" (XI, 19, 1). It is as though one were listening to a novice who, in the ardor of his new-found piety, can scarcely bear to receive visits from his family. Every morning Lucius is the first one there, waiting for the temple doors to open.[54] The white curtains have hardly been pulled aside from the statue of Isis before he, with the other worshipers, is invoking her (XI, 20, 4). But when the others depart, he remains, contemplating the goddess in sweet peace of soul, meditating and keeping exemplary silence the whole day long.[55] These transports of piety redouble after the initiation: "After that I remained there a few more days, deriving an ineffable pleasure from the image of the goddess. I was under such obligation to her that I could never hope to repay the debt." (XI, 24, 5.) When at last Isis herself tells him to return home, it is with great difficulty that he makes up his mind to leave her: "And so, with the greatest difficulty snapping the bonds of my most ardent desire, I made ready for the journey home. At the last I cast myself to the ground before the goddess and spent a long time drying with my face the tears I shed on her feet; then in speech barely articulate and punctuated by sobs I prayed to her." (XI, 24, 6–7.) There follows a kind of liturgical hymn (XI, 25, 2–5) of the most artful composition, which is a little surprising at this moment of extreme emotion;[56] however, the rhetorician is bound to reveal himself from time to time. The prayer ends by this rather touching promise (XI, 25, 5–6): "My intellect is not strong enough to tell thy praises; my patrimony is too small for me to offer sacrifices; my voice hath not the richness to utter that which I think of Thy majesty, no, not if I had a thousand mouths and as many tongues and were able to continue for ever. So I shall try the only thing which a devotee, though poor in all else, can: I shall always keep Thy divine appearance and Thy most holy godhead locked in the privacy of my heart and shall conjure them up in my imagination."

Now this contemplative adoration is somewhat peculiar. It was no doubt quite common in Greece for those visiting a sanctuary to admire the sculptures in the temple, and to ask the sacristan for an interpretation of them. So Pausanias did during his journeys through Greece in the second century of our era. Still earlier we have the charming little scene in the *Ion* of Euripides. It is morning in the sanctuary of Delphi. A group of women arrive—they are the servants of Creusa—and are lost in admiration before the sculptures of the temple.[57] An analogous scene is described for us by Herodas in his fourth mime, the *Women at the Temple of Asclepius* (at Cos). But it is a far cry from this superficial curiosity of the laity to the contemplative adoration of Lucius before the statue of Isis. The difference is the same as that which separates a band of summer tourists visiting the Cathedral of Chartres from the poor woman who prays for long hours before the statue of Our Lady in the crypt of that church.

There is no doubt, too, that the ancients were not insensible to the religious values embodied in certain cult statues, for example, the Zeus of Phidias at Olympia. It is enough to recall the famous *Olympian Discourse* of Dio Chrysostom.[58] However, there is still a great deal of difference between the aesthetic analysis of the religious elements present in a work of art, as, for example, any given famous medieval statue of the Virgin, and the losing of oneself in loving contemplation of the divine person or saint whom it represents. From the Hellenistic Age on, the ancients practiced art criticism. The case of Lucius, however, remains an isolated example.

L osing oneself in contemplation of divine image

In Egypt likewise, it was common enough to go on a pilgrimage, often to a far-off sanctuary, in order to consult a holy and oracular statue.[59] Such a statue was thought to be alive. For example, it nodded its head in response to the question asked of it; or else a voice issued from it. These effects were obtained by some mechanical device. On other occasions, the rays of the rising sun would strike the face of the statue, which would then appear animated and glorified. Yet, here too there is no direct connection with the *inexplicabilis voluptas* which Lucius feels in the presence of the statue of Isis. The pilgrim visiting Mandoulis-Aiôn came to consult the god for a definite purpose. When he had obtained the answer he sought for, he left. He did not establish himself in the temple, nor live there in order to be all the time in loving union with his god. He was not *cultor assiduus*, *cultor inseparabilis*. In a word, his prayer was not disinterested. Lucius' contemplation has no end beyond itself. He asks nothing. His whole happiness consists in gazing upon his Beloved.

There is also no analogy to be found with the Greek mysteries, such as the Eleusinian. The hierophant there unveiled and displayed sacred objects (*hiera*), and this exposition undoubtedly played a role of capital importance in the initiation, for it marked the climax and conclusion of the ceremony; the *epoptae* of the Great Eleusinian Mysteries are, as their very name shows, people who have *seen*. Nevertheless, the exposition was only a brief act in the ceremony. It represented a pledge to the faithful, who could respond with more or less enthusiasm, each man according to his temperament. But that was all. Nobody settled down in the sanctuary to be always close to the *hiera*. Nobody lingered to gaze upon them lovingly. Besides, there is nothing to indicate that the sacred objects were especially made for loving contemplation.

No text of pagan antiquity, therefore, affords an exact parallel to Apuleius' description. How, then, are we to explain Lucius' intense emotion in the presence of his divine friend? For my part, I believe it to be a phenomenon of religious psychology, and therein lies its interest.

Felt
love
&
Loved
in
return

Lucius feels that he is loved. He believes in the love of Isis.
This faith of his is absolute. How could he *not* be loved by Isis,
when she herself sought him out in his misery (let us recall that
it was not to Isis, but to whatever goddess showed herself in the
moon, that he had addressed his prayer at Cenchreae), when
she appeared to him in her own form, and, by a wondrous miracle, restored him to his man's shape, and, thereafter, guided
him every night by her counsel? Now we observe here a very
interesting psychological phenomenon. Lucius is, of course, a
fictitious character. Apuleius, however, is not; he is a genuine
historical figure. In order to paint his hero's state of soul with
so much warmth, with such accents of truth, he must himself
have known that spiritual condition. We therefore find ourselves obliged to admit that certain pagans thought themselves
really loved by this or that divine personage drawn from the old
national religions. This realization must cause us to reflect,
and perhaps to revise our opinions. After all, religious feeling
does not change. Man feels an invincible need to believe that
there is somewhere a God who thinks about him, who loves
him—loves him as he is, impure and wretched. It was the
humble of this world who first believed in the religion of Christ:
slaves, Corinthian dockers, the sinful woman of the Gospel—
soiled, degraded beings. It did not seem amazing to them that
a God should come on earth to seek them, and to save them.
Was it so astonishing that this God should truly love them? Recalling this attitude on the part of the early generations of
Christians, and making all the appropriate distinctions, we
come to understand better the exaltation of Lucius. He felt
himself loved. He loved in return. It was because of these
things that he found in the contemplation of his Goddess an
ineffable joy. (See our frontispiece.)

VI

Popular Piety

Aelius Aristides and Asclepius

HAD Aelius Aristides not written his *Sacred Discourses*, and the Roman speech, he would be a fairly commonplace person of little interest for us. He was what in the second century of our era was called a *sophistes*, which meant an orator traveling from city to city and delivering, or rather reading, set speeches of divers sorts: the panegyric of a god or of a city, or a declamation on some literary or ethical commonplace.[1]

All this sort of thing is idle and empty enough, and today Aristides is not very readable,[2] no more readable than his contemporary Maximus of Tyre, another "itinerant lecturer." I should be inclined to match this genre of Sophistical speeches under the Empire with the set sermon which, up to a few years ago, was common in certain countries of Europe. If there was a celebration in a cathedral, say of the installation of new bells or a new organ, or the feast of the patron saint of the cathedral— often a martyr of whom next to nothing was known,—a famous preacher was sent for, who would expatiate pompously on some insipid commonplace: the salutary effect of music, the beauties of liturgical worship, the greatness of the martyr in question. These floods of eloquence have not been preserved—for which we may be thankful, since our taste has altered. But the ancients took great pleasure in qualities of form, regardless of how trite and devoid of meaning the content of a speech might be. To understand, and perhaps to excuse, Aristides, one has only to read Philostratus' *Lives of the Sophists*, or to imagine what the circle of Pliny the Younger was like at Rome half a century earlier. But fortunately Aristides wrote his six *Sacred Discourses*,[3] a unique document and one of the most remarkable of antiquity.

85

Let us imagine a sick man who places all his confidence not in a doctor, but in a god. The god appears before him at night, gives him directions, usually paradoxical, which amount to a series of ordeals. That he may be closer to the god, the sick man takes up his residence in the sanctuary itself, just as today a man might move to a spa or to a sanatorium near by. The sick man obeys all orders blindly; and, since the imagination plays a large part in certain chronic illnesses, particularly when the patient is of a nervous temperament, the orders actually do him good, bodily and especially mentally. They help him; but he is not cured. Better say: they help him, and therefore he is not cured, because fundamentally he does not want to be cured. To be cured would mean no longer to enjoy the presence and companionship of the god; and precisely what the patient needs most is the companionship of the god. The patient must continually have attention paid to him. The god tells him to do things which would soon make an end of an ordinary man. The sick man not only survives these things, but thrives on them. The more unheard-of the treatment, the more the patient is convinced that the god is interested in his case, that his case is a special one, and that he is the most privileged being on the face of the earth. Thus he comes to be no longer able to do without the god, and by the same token to be no longer able to do without his sickness.

Furthermore, the god signifies more for him than the physician of his body; he directs him spiritually as well. He tells him whether he should work or not, and to what sort of work he should put his hand; he encourages him by comparing him to the finest orators of antiquity, to Alexander the Great himself, and by comparing him to a god. He sends him to speak in this or that city; he upholds him in his disputes with rivals; he becomes his perpetual counselor, directing him in all the details of his existence.

Let us finally imagine that in the sanctuary where the sick man has made his lodgings, he is not alone; there are other patients also, whose treatment is the same: they await nocturnal visions wherein the god will prescribe a remedy. During the day these patients, who are men of wealth, distinction, and leisure, spend their time as people spend theirs now in sanatoriums and at watering places, talking about their illnesses and their treatments. Since the doctor is a god, and since it is by visions that he treats them, they compare these visions. "He told *me* . . . ," "Well, he told *me* . . . ," etc. All day long in this way they keep themselves in a state of religious excitement, a state which brings them dreams at night. Then the next day, like the day before, is spent in interpreting the dreams, in comparing them, or in watching the performances the god has imposed on someone or other of their company; and all this is combined with visits to the temple, with conversations with the priest or the sacristans, and also with literary discussions. For this small society is a cultivated one; its members write, show each other what they have written, encourage and flatter each other. Truly a strange milieu, lively, gossiping, amusing, in certain ways amazingly modern! So one still sees today, in certain health resorts, around some famous doctor, the same mixture of dazzled admiration for him, of unconditional obedience to his orders, and of the spirit of a philosophical and literary coterie. Poor Katherine Mansfield died in a sanatorium near Paris very much like the sanctuary of Pergamum.

Such is the scene and such are the characters whom we come to know in the *Hieroi Logoi* or *Sacred Discourses* of Aristides; and they make the book delightful reading. But another cause, too, contributes to this; whereas Aristides' set speeches are written in a highly elaborate, often ornate prose, of the sort which ancients loved but which we find dull as dishwater, the *Sacred Discourses* are written slapdash, in a style which is simple, rapid, at times even incorrect, yet always delightful, because it is the work of a born writer, who has animation and sparkle. Aristides is like Cicero, whose great speeches may bore us, while his letters never fail to charm. Unfortunately, all the work of Aristides has fallen under the same discredit. To my knowledge, there exists no modern translation of the *Hieroi*

Logoi. I shall here attempt to fill this gap in some measure by quoting a few passages.

First a word on the title, *Hieroi Logoi*. The Greeks meant by *Hieros Logos* in the true sense of the word a sacred legend justifying a rite of special worship, such as a sacred interdiction or a ceremony of initiation. A good example is given us by Pausanias (VIII 15, 1 ff.) concerning the sanctuary of Demeter in Pheneus in Arcadia. "The Pheneates had a legend (*logos*) that Demeter came to Pheneus on her wanderings, and that to those who welcomed her hospitably she gave all the different kinds of pulse except beans" (VIII 15, 3). Pausanias adds: "They have a sacred story about the bean to show why they think it an unclean kind of pulse."[4] Generally this precept or interdiction was a divine revelation, made in the course of an apparition or epiphany, whether the divinity came by day and as a creature of flesh and blood—as in the Pheneus legend, which is copied from that current at Eleusis—or whether by night in a dream-vision. Thus *Hieros Logos* may be translated as: "An account of the apparition of a god or goddess who makes a revelation." This fits the *Sacred Discourses* or *Sacred Stories* of Aristides perfectly: he recounts visions of Asclepius (or of Sarapis, or of Isis) in which the god makes revelations to him.[5]

Let us turn to the *Sacred Stories*. First I shall give you a few indications of the nature of Aristides' illness. Then we shall consider the revelations of Asclepius, those of a medical kind as well as those which belong more specially to the domain of religion. In conclusion I shall attempt to define the nature of Aristides' religious experience.

ARISTIDES' ILLNESS

Probably born in 117 A.D. in Hadrianutherae, a city of Mysia,[6] Aelius Aristides, about December of the year 143, set out for Rome. He was then twenty-seven years of age, had made serious studies in rhetoric at Cotiaeum and in Athens (under Herodes Atticus), and had tried out his talents in Egypt (in 142). Rome was bound to attract him. It was to Rome that the

Sophists—Dio Chrysostom, Maximus of Tyre, Apuleius—went to seek the official sanction of their renown. Aristides had just been through a cure at the warm springs near the Aesepus in the Troad. This cure had tired him;[7] and besides, he had caught cold. Nevertheless he left. He traveled in a coach, with several servants, by the land route, the *Via Egnatia*, through Thrace and Macedonia to Dyrrhachium, where travelers took ship for Brundisium.

We need not set forth in detail the highly picturesque account of this journey (XLVIII 60–68 K., XXIV 304 ff. D.). Suffice it to say that it was ghastly. It was midwinter, the roads were abominable, and it was then that Aristides began to suffer from his illness or illnesses: toothaches; earaches; most of all, fits of asthma and attacks of fever. At Edessa (present-day Vodena) he was forced to take to his bed, and did not reach Rome until a hundred days after he had set out; that is, about March, 144. At Rome his condition did not improve: "My stomach was bloated, my muscles were cramped, shivers ran up and down my body, it was impossible to breathe." In the second century, even in Rome, medicine was in its infancy. Purges, cupping by scarification, antidotes, and other remedies of every sort,[8] availed him nothing. "Everything was incurable, there was not the shadow of a hope." So it was decided to take Aristides back to Smyrna, this time by sea since he no longer had the strength to endure the jolting of the carriage. But the sea voyage was no better, and Aristides had to suffer through shaking, tossing, squalls and storm. Finally, toward the end of autumn he landed in Miletus, and from there went on to Smyrna.

This was the winter of 144 and 145. Aristides stayed in Smyrna more than a year before he went to the sanctuary of Asclepius in Pergamum, in the spring of 146. This is how he describes his illnesses (XLVIII 5–7 K., XXIV 292 D.):

"When I had been brought back from Italy, having collected in my body many ailments of every sort as a result of the continued hardships and storms which I had had to endure while traveling through Thrace and Macedonia (and I was already ill when I started out), the doctors were at a loss: not only could they think of nothing to help me, but they were not even able to recognize what was wrong with me to begin with. The most painful and distressing part of it was that I could not breathe; only with the greatest difficulty at times and with a dread that I might not succeed was I able to draw breath, and then only heavily and barely enough. My throat was constantly being choked up; shivers ran through the sinews of my body; I needed more covers than I could stand. And there were countless other things wrong with me. They thought I should try the hot baths; they might make my condition better, or else I might find the atmosphere more supportable. It was already wintertime, and the baths were not far from the city.

"That was when the Savior first began to give me revelations. He ordered me to walk barefoot, and I cried out in my dream as if I were wide awake and the vision had been carried out: 'Great is Asclepius! the order has been fulfilled!' That was what I dreamed I cried out while walking forward. After this came the god's invitation and my departure from Smyrna to Pergamum to my good fortune."

Further on, in order to make yet more evident the healing power of the god, Aristides gives us a whole catalogue of his illnesses (XLVIII 56–58 K., XXIV 303 D.): "What man could conceive of the multitude of ills of which I was then a victim? Those who were present on the occasion of each attack know the state of my skin and how sick I was internally. Moreover, my head ran with mucus day after day and night after night; there was fluxion in my chest; my breath would come up to meet the flow of humors in my throat, would be constricted and become inflamed there. I was so much expecting death from minute to minute that I did not have the courage to call a slave; I thought I should be wasting my time, because it would be too late by the time he came. On top of all this, I had every kind of trouble with my ears and my teeth, and tension round about the veins, and I could neither keep down what I had eaten nor throw it up; for if anything so much as touched my throat or my palate,

it closed all the passages, and I could not recover myself. I had
a burning pain inside my head and every kind of shooting fits.
At night I was unable to lie down flat; I had to keep sitting up
bent forward, my head resting on my knees. In the grip of such
ills as these and an infinity of others, I had of course to keep
myself wrapped up in woolen blankets and other kinds of covers
and be entirely confined with all doors and windows closed, so
that the day came to equal the night, and the nights were like
days because I could not sleep."[9]

THE MEDICAL PRESCRIPTIONS OF ASCLEPIUS

The illnesses of Aristides were many and various, and so was the
treatment which the god prescribed to him. He speaks of balms, ·
of poultices, of a diet (sometimes complete fasting, sometimes
this or that food or beverage), of warm baths, of purges, of
bloodlettings. But in particular he describes three varieties of
external treatment: going barefoot, riding horseback, and cold
baths, the very ones which Marcus Aurelius mentions as the
usual orders of Asclepius (V 8, 1): "We commonly say (τὸ
λεγόμενον): Asclepius prescribed to someone horseback riding,
or cold baths, or going barefoot." Certain of these remedies and
exercises had long been known to Greek medicine and Greek
hygiene. Diocles of Carystus (at the end of the fourth century
B.C.) recommends cold baths (ψυχρολουσία) to consumptives.[10]
Walking barefoot in winter or early in the morning was a hard-
ening exercise practiced from of old by the Spartan youth[11] and
by the Pythagoreans.[12] Again, these same remedies as prescriptions of Asclepius are found in other documents of Imperial
times. Under the reign of Antoninus Pius, Apellas of Mylasa is
sent by Asclepius to Epidaurus for his health, and there receives
the order to take walks barefoot.[13] Speaking of maladies caused
by want of measure in the movements of the soul, Galen says:
"Asclepius ordered not a few to write odes as well as to compose
comical mimes and certain songs (for the motions of their
passions, having become more vehement, had made the temperature of the body warmer than it should be); and for others,

these not a few either, he ordered hunting and horseback riding and exercising in arms; for he desired to awake the passion of these men because it was weak."[14] One cannot say, then, that Aristides' case was entirely original. But what gives these orders their paradoxical, miraculous, and therefore divine character is that the exercises, painful and violent enough in themselves, were prescribed to Aristides when his sickness was at its worst and he could hardly stand upright. He himself notes the miraculous character of his cures in his *Lalia to Asclepius* (XLII 8 K., VI 38 f. D.):[15] "Indeed it is the paradoxical which predominates in the cures of the god; for example, one drinks chalk, another hemlock, another one strips off his clothes and takes cold baths, when it is warmth, and not at all cold, that one would think he is in need of.[16] Now myself he has likewise distinguished in this way, stopping catarrhs and colds by baths in rivers and in the sea, healing me through long walks when I was helplessly bed-ridden, administering terrible purgations on top of continuous abstinence from food, prescribing that I should speak and write when I could hardly breathe, so that if any justification for boasting should fall to those who have been healed in such a way, we certainly have our share in this boast."[17]

Walking barefoot is recommended to Aristides by Asclepius in his very first appearance in a dream (XLVIII 7 K., XXIV 292 D.): "Then it was that for the first time the Savior began to give me revelations. He ordered me to go about barefoot." This exercise is mentioned (XLVIII 80 K., XXIV 308 f. D.) as one of the usual orders of the god: "Akin to these [cold baths], there was going barefoot continually in the middle of winter, and there were nights spent in all parts of the sanctuary, in the open air and anywhere, particularly in the temple way beneath the sacred lamp of the goddess [Hygeia] itself." Walking barefoot is associated with horseback riding as a remedy for tumors. Let us quote this curious account in full (XLVII 61–65 K., XXIII 287 f. D.): "So much for my abdomen. I had a similar experience with a tumor some years previously. The god had forewarned me that I should guard myself with the utmost care against dropsy, and among other antidotes prescribed Egyptian shoes, of the sort which the priests wear.[18] He had decided in particular that the flow of humors should be drawn off from beneath. Then I got a tumor from no evident cause, at first such as anyone might get; but then it grew to enormous size. My groin was full of pus, and everything was swollen. There followed terrible pains and a fever for some days. The doctors gave all sorts of opinions. Some would have it removed by incision, others wanted caustic preparations to be applied as the only way to keep me from becoming infected beneath the surface, which would be fatal. But the god gave a contrary opinion, that I should hold out and let it grow. Clearly, between obeying the doctors and obeying the god there was no choice. The tumor grew yet more and I was in much distress. Some of my friends admired my endurance; others accused me of going to excess in placing all my confidence in dreams; some blamed me for a coward, since I would neither allow the thing to be cut off nor take any drug. But the god stood firm to the end, telling me to put up with my present troubles, since it was all with a view to my health. The reason he gave was that the springs of this flow were above, and that these 'gardeners' did not know which way to divert the streams. Well, the outcome was extraordinary. I went on like this for about four months. During all this time my head and the upper part of my abdomen were as clear and comfortable as one could have wished. . . . I was ordered to do many paradoxical things; among those which I recall there is a race which I had to run barefoot in wintertime, and again horseback riding, the most arduous of undertakings; and I also recall an exercise of the following kind: when the harbor waves were swollen by the south wind and ships were in distress, I had to sail across to the opposite side, eating honey and acorns from an oak tree, and vomit; then complete purgation was achieved. All these things were done when the inflammation was at its peak and had even risen to the navel."[19]

Here is another example of cure by riding on horseback (XLIX 3–5 K., XXV 310 D.): "While I was sick at Alliani, I remember having a dream something like this: I thought I was sailing on a small boat in the Egyptian sea, alone. I was on the highest part of the boat, on the part turned landward. While I was there and suffering from my illness, my foster-father Zosimus appeared to me (on the dry land) with a horse; and somehow I left the ship and seized the horse with joy. Such was the dream. . . . When the day came, I had a horse at hand, and mounted instantly, I whom no one would have thought to have the strength even to start out; I ran him at a gallop, and began to feel better the more he ran. Much of the pain in the upper part of my body left me, and in the circumstances a sense of power gathered in me. I began to have hopes again. Then in the night I heard a voice saying: 'Thy cure is complete!' And all this was when I was at the most desperate juncture."

Finally, here is a description of one of the many cold baths prescribed by Asclepius. Aristides carried out this performance in the river Meletas, which runs close to Smyrna (XLVIII 19–23 K., XXIV 295 D.): "It was in the depths of winter. There was a bitter wind from the north, and frost. The pebbles were so glued together by the frost as to look like a network of crystal, and the water was what one would expect it to be in such a climate. When the manifestation of the god was made known, my friends came with me, also some doctors who knew me well, and others, some anxious on my account, some out of scientific curiosity. There was a great crowd besides, for there happened to be a distribution of largess (διάδοσις)[20] outside the gates, and everything could be seen very well from the bridge. There was a doctor named Heracleon, a friend of mine, who confessed to me the next day that he had come convinced that at the very best I should be seized by a tetanic recurvation (ὀπισθοτόνῳ) or something similar. When I came to the river, I had no need of any encouragement. Still full of the warmth of the vision of the god, I tore off my clothes, and, without even asking for a rubdown, jumped into the deepest part of the river. Then, just as if I were in a pool of mild water of just the right temperature, I took my time swimming and splashing about. When I came

out, my skin was fresh and shining, my body was perfectly
light, and the whole crowd of those who had come with me and
those who had come later gave forth in splendid volume the
famous cry: 'Great is Asclepius!' Who could describe what
followed? All the rest of that day and in the evening until I
went to bed I remained in the state in which I had come out
of the bath; I did not feel my body to be drier, or any wetter;
the warmth which I felt did not leave me, nor was any added
to it; nor did this warmth seem to be such as any human
device might have brought about; it was a sort of continuous
animal warmth, of equal strength throughout all my limbs and
over the whole surface of the body. I was in a corresponding
state mentally. It was not an obvious pleasure, nor would you
have measured it by the standards of ordinary human good
cheer. Rather it was a certain indescribable sense of well-being
which made all things seem of secondary importance beside the
present moment, so that not even when I saw something did I
have the impression that I was seeing it—so wholly close was I
to the god."[21]

RELIGIOUS REVELATIONS

Asclepius' revelations dealt with more than Aristides' state of
bodily health. There was a whole series intended to encourage
our author's rhetorical career and his literary production (L 13–
47 K., XXVI 323 ff. D.). More interesting for our present purpose are those revelations which may be called properly religious; that is, those which the god made about himself or about
his relations with his devotee.

First let us read some visions concerning the close union of
the god and Aristides (L 50–52 K., XXVI 333 D.): "Now let
what follows, if it is permitted, be said and written; if it is not
permitted, do thou take care, lord Asclepius, to dispose me to
erase it without any hard feeling. First I saw the statue with
three heads;[22] a flame illuminated it all round, except for the
heads. Then we, the god's devotees, came forward, just as when
the paean is being sung. And I was almost in the front row. At
that point the god gave the sign of dismissal; he was now in the

form in which we see him in his statues. All the others began to go, and I too turned round to go with them, when the god beckoned to me to stay. And I, in ecstasy over the honor done me, and over my being chosen above all the rest, cried out: 'One alone!'—meaning of course the god; whereupon he said: 'You are that.'[23] This utterance, O my lord Asclepius, is worth more to me than all this mortal life; no sickness, no joy comes up to it; it has given me both the will and the strength to live. . . .

"I once heard from the god the following remark concerning my talks and my conversance with the god: he said that my mind was to be rapt from my present state of life; that when it was so rapt, I should be made one with God, and being made one with God, I should have transcended our mortal state; he said that neither the circumstance that, being one with God, I should have transcended the mortal state, nor the circumstance that, having transcended the mortal state, I should be one with God, should cause me the least surprise."

There follows a dream-vision in which Asclepius reveals himself to Aristides as the World-Soul of Plato (L 55–56 K., XXVI 334 D.): "The god also made me a revelation of his nature, partly to the eye, partly even to the ear. This is how it was. When the dream took place, the morning star was rising on the horizon, and I dreamt that I was walking along a certain path on my estate toward the star, which had just come up (I was walking eastward). Pyrallianus from the temple was with me; he is a friend of mine and well versed in the dialogues of Plato. As is natural when one is on a walk and at leisure, I said to him jokingly and to tease him: 'Look here, we're alone now and no one can hear us; can you, in heaven's name, tell me why all this mummery about Plato by which you so impress everybody?' I was aiming the question at the discussions on nature and on ultimate reality. He told me to follow him and to pay close attention. From then on, he led and I followed. He went forward a little bit, held up his hand, and pointed to a certain spot in the sky; at the same time he said: 'That's the one Plato calls the Soul of the Universe.' I looked, and saw Asclepius of Pergamum enthroned in the sky; and at that point I woke up and saw that it was the same hour that it had been in my dream."[24]

It would also be interesting to quote the vision of the underworld which Aristides one day received from Sarapis.[25] But although even in this passage Aristides presents Sarapis ". . . as in a manner resembling Asclepius," yet it *is* Sarapis, and not Asclepius, who has granted him these revelations of the world beyond. The reason is, as Edelstein has rightly pointed out,[26] that ". . . the god of medicine himself had nothing to tell about the life to come; as a physician it was not his task to concern himself with the beyond; in saving men, he was concerned with this world." Let us indicate only what sort of feelings Aristides had in the presence of his god (XLVIII 31–33 K., XXIV 298 D.): "It [sc. the remedy] was revealed in the clearest way possible, just as countless other things also made the presence of the god manifest. For I seemed as it were to touch him and to perceive that he himself was come, and to be halfway between sleep and waking and to want to get the power of vision and to be anxious lest he depart beforehand, and to have applied my ears and to hear, sometimes as in a dream, sometimes as in a waking vision, and my hair was standing on end and tears of joy came forth, and the consciousness I had of his weighty presence was no burden—what man could even set these things forth in words? But if he is one of the initiates, then he knows and understands."[27]

Aristides' Religious Experience

We have yet to deal with what is most important. How is this complete confidence of Aristides in Asclepius to be explained? Let us begin by making two observations.

In the first place, it is impossible to doubt for an instant the sincerity of Aristides. One cannot be fond of him. He is incredibly vain, profoundly egotistical. Persuaded that on two occasions Asclepius prolonged his life by causing to die in his place the young son Hermias (XLVIII 37–44 K.) and the young daughter Philumene (LI 18–25 K.) of his foster-sister Callityche

(LI 25 K.), he has no word of pity for these children, but finds the substitution quite natural since he is himself the favorite of the god. Besides, it may seem rather disturbing that these intimate bonds between Aristides and his god have no greater result than consultations to determine whether he should bathe or take a purge. However, these faults of the man and his smallness of spirit do not fundamentally change the problem in the least. What we have here is a remarkable example of personal religion, of personal attachment to a divinity. It is of little importance what the union leads to; what counts is the fact of the union. It must be admitted that Aristides believed with all his soul in the benevolent friendship of Asclepius. It must also be admitted that he rendered the god absolute obedience, even when his orders might well seem extravagant or painful.

In the second place, one remark must be made concerning the mode of delivery of the god's prescriptions. These prescriptions are delivered in dreams. As the result of dreams he has had at night, Aristides persuades himself that the god is prescribing this or that remedy, sending him to this or that place, exhorting him to, or dissuading him from, this or that enterprise. Now at the first glance there is a factual impossibility in all this. Even granted an imagination overexcited and entirely directed to a single object, it is inconceivable that the same person should have the same dream night after night; for example, that Aristides should have seen every night the god in person giving him some order. The truth is, as the *Sacred Discourses* make abundantly clear, that Aristides' dreams were widely diverse. But he himself interpreted them in the morning as divine ordinances. Thus it is by no means the dreams that led to his faith in the god, but rather his faith in the god which determined his interpretation of the dreams. The faith comes first. A further distinction must be drawn between that common belief which Aristides must have shared with nearly all his contemporaries and that total faith, that utter abandonment of self which, after a certain point, we see that Aristides renders to the god. In other words, different periods must be distinguished. First, there was a period of common belief. Then, at a certain moment, there was a sort of crisis, followed by an act of absolute faith. From this time on, Aristides' entire life was changed, and he became the witness to Asclepius whom we know from the *Sacred Discourses*. It is interesting to follow this evolution, which leads us to the heart of the problem.

Long before he fell ill himself, Aristides already believed in the healing power of Asclepius. It was the common belief of the day. Aristides had been raised in the traditional religion; his father Eudaemon was the priest of a sanctuary of Zeus near the family estate. Aristides' hymns to the gods prove that he faithfully observed the piety of his fathers. Yet these hymns themselves, in perfect conformity with the standard phraseology, reveal not the slightest trace of personal religion. Further, as Wilamowitz has noted with great penetration,[28] there is in them no trace of any special devotion to Asclepius. In the *Hymn to Zeus*, written before his great illness, the true deliverer is Zeus,[29] and Asclepius makes his appearance, together with Apollo, Athene, Hera, and Artemis, as a mere subordinate of Zeus, who "heals those whom Zeus would have healed."[30] In the *Hymn to Sarapis*, which was probably recited at Smyrna shortly after the return of Aristides from Egypt,[31] Asclepius is not even mentioned—whereas later he will be described as almost like Sarapis,[32]—and here it is Sarapis who is the healer of the body and who gives men health.[33] These expressions clearly do not exclude a belief in the powers of Asclepius; after all, according to the usage of the time and the traditions of this literary genre, it was normal to attribute to the divinity who is being honored the greatest possible number of qualities; nonetheless, Asclepius is not in the first rank. Furthermore, the conventional tone of the hymns is quite different from that of the *Sacred Discourses*.

Therefore there was a crisis, and it is not difficult to determine its date and its causes. Aristides had been very ill, first at Rome, and then, after his return from Rome, at Smyrna, where he remained for a year longer. Now, in the course of this illness, he turned at first not to Asclepius, but to doctors.[34] These doctors, both at Rome and at Smyrna, gave up his case; they could not even tell what was wrong with him, and they left the patient to his own devices.[35] In short, the crisis came about in Smyrna after the voyage to Rome, and its reason was the utter discouragement of Aristides when the doctors gave up his case as hopeless. They had sent him to the Warm Springs near Smyrna in the faint hope that he would feel better there.[36] "Then it was," he tells us—probably right there at the Warm Springs,— "that the Savior first began to give me revelations."[37] It was natural that, in such an extremity, Aristides must have been thinking for some time of having recourse to the greatest Doctor of them all, whose cult was then so widespread in Asia Minor.[38] It was natural that other men who had been afflicted with disease and then cured by the god should have recommended a pilgrimage to Pergamum. In desperate cases, Asclepius remained the only hope.[39] Finally, Aristides had a dream, which he did not hesitate to interpret as a divine order. The remedy prescribed—to walk barefoot—was very much in line with the usual orders of the god. Then Aristides uttered in his dream the liturgical acclamation which is the typical expression of the act of faith: "Great is Asclepius!"[40] He awoke not a healthy man— that was never to be,—but the passionate devotee of Asclepius.

There was the crisis, and there began the new life. From now on, Aristides belongs to his god and obeys him and him alone. One day (XLIX 8–9 K., XXV 311 D.), while bedridden in Pergamum, he receives a visit from a famous doctor, Satyrus. Aristides had just undergone a series of bleedings which had left him exhausted. Satyrus, having felt his chest and abdomen, recommended that the bleedings be stopped and prescribed a poultice. "I answered him," says Aristides, "that I was not master of my blood to do with it as I wished, but that as long as the god ordered me to be bled, I would obey whether I wanted to or not—or rather, it was impossible for me ever not to want to."[41] He says even more in another passage (XLVIII 73 K., XXIV 307 D.): "For the very same regimen and the very same things which, when the god was their author and explicitly commanded them, brought health, strength, agility, comfort, a sense of well-being, all the best things both for the body and for the spirit, had precisely the opposite effect if another recommended them without guessing at the mind of the god." Is that not, asks Aristides in conclusion, the strongest proof of the power of Asclepius?

What it proves in any case is the unshakable faith of Aristides. This faith, once given, explains everything else. As soon as one has thoroughly persuaded oneself that every dream must contain a message from the divine, it remains only to interpret the dreams in this sense. The ancients, in the second century of our era, were past masters in the pseudo-science of dream interpretation (*onirocrisia*). At the very time when Aristides lived, and in the same province of Asia, Artemidorus of Ephesus composed his *Treatise on the Interpretation of Dreams* (*Onirocriticon*) in five books, the summation of a long tradition. In it he expounded the rules and methods of *onirocrisia*, all based on this principle: "*Onirocrisia* is nothing other than the passage from the likely to the likely."[42]

So all Aristides had to do each morning was to apply these rules to the dreams of the night before. If he dreams, while returning from Hadrianutherae to Pergamum, that someone brings him a book of Menander, he concludes that he must stay (*menein*) where he is, and not continue the voyage (XLVII 51 K.). There is a similar occurrence another time, when he is returning from Cyzicus to Smyrna in the winter. The first day has been reasonably mild, and that night he dreams that he is holding a copy of the *Clouds* of Aristophanes in his hands. That means that they must halt at that night's resting place. As a matter of fact, the next day *is* cloudy, and it begins to rain (LI 18 K.). Or again, being seized by a tertian fever, he dreams that Lysias (the Deliverer) appears to him in the form of a gracious youth. This is a sign that he will be delivered from the fever (Λυσίας : ἐλύθη τὸ νόσημα), and it finally does leave him (L 59 K.). One night he dreams that a bone is stuck in his throat and that he must disgorge it. That gives him the idea of having blood let from his ankles (XLVII 28 K.). If he dreams that he sees Athena bearing the aegis, as Phidias represented her at Athens, he immediately infers that he must wash himself in *Attic* honey (XLVIII 40–43 K.). Sometimes the dream is ambiguous and admits of two interpretations; for example, the dream in which Aristides imagines that he is in Smyrna, that he eats some figs, learns that they contain poison, and immediately vomits. Once awake, he wonders: should I fast or vomit? The matter stands in need of elucidation, and Aristides begs Asclepius to indicate his wishes more clearly. The next night, he dreams that he is in Pergamum fasting. Theodotus, the doctor, comes up to him, approves his fasting, and gives his opinion against bloodletting. "Your pain lies in the kidney," he tells him, "and fasting is a sort of bastard way out for the fire through the chest." At the same instant, Aristides sees two sparks in front of him. Theodotus explains to him: "That comes from this fire." The fire, then, is really gone, which means that the god prescribed fasting and forbids bloodletting. Aristides wakes up, and a doctor comes to bleed him; Aristides tells him his dream, and the doctor has the good sense to yield to the god. "And I," says Aristides, "I recognized the true Doctor and the only one to treat my illness; and I did as he ordered. After that I passed the night with perfect ease, and had no pain whatsoever." (XLVII 54–58 K., XXIII 285 D.)

In cases of doubt, Aristides may also tell his dreams to friends to ask their advice. He does this especially at Pergamum, where he is living in the sanctuary itself and in contact with the personnel of the temple, who are accustomed to solve such problems. There is the occasion, for example, when Aristides is hesitating to take a draught of wormwood recommended by the god. "Having seen these things in the night, I called the physician Theodotus when morning dawned, and described to him my dreams. He was astonished at their strangeness, and he was at a loss what to make of them, since it was wintertime, and besides, he was anxious over the great weakness of my body; for I had already been confined to my home for many months. For this reason it seemed to us to be a good idea to summon the sacristan Asclepiacus as well. I was then living in his house, and I was in the habit of communicating to him many of my dreams." Asclepiacus then arrives, and tells him that his colleague Philadelphus has had that very night a dream which concerns Aristides directly. They call for Philadelphus, who tells his dream, and Aristides swallows the wormwood without hesitation (XLVIII 34–35 K., XXIV 298 D.). Besides, as I have said above, this whole little devout society of Pergamum spent its days comparing diseases and remedies. One day when there was a celebration in the town (Pergamum), Aristides found himself alone in the sanctuary with a distinguished personage of senatorial rank named Sedatus. "We were sitting there in the temple of Hygeia, near the statue of Telesphorus," says Aristides, "and we were asking each other, as usual, if the god had prescribed anything out of the ordinary to either of us; for our illnesses had a good deal in common" (L 16 K., XXVI 324 D.).

If one takes into consideration all these facts—(1) the unconditional faith in the god, (2) the ancient and common practice of dream interpretation, (3) this rather special society of impressionable patients, living in the constant expectation of some medical order more paradoxical than those that had gone before, and (4) the personnel of the temple accustomed to this clientele of neuropaths, and well-versed in the interpretation of dreams, though there is no reason to accuse them of charlatanry, since, after all, the sacristans and priests of Pergamum could believe in the power of Asclepius as well as anyone else—if one takes all these things into account, Aristides' case seems less extraordinary. Finally, when dealing with the ancients, we must always keep in mind an important difference between the ancient and the modern religious psychology. Since we have a far higher concept of the Divinity, the notion of habitual communication between God and man seems to us unlikely. We live, generally, in a rationalist atmosphere, and when we are in need of help we usually rely on human means. In this respect, ancient man is much closer than modern man to the divine. To him it seems entirely natural that the gods should mingle with human beings. The men of Lystra, a town of Lycaonia, in Asia Minor, believe spontaneously that Zeus and Hermes have come down from heaven to their small town (Act. Apost. 14: 12). Artemidorus devotes several chapters (II, 34–41) to divine apparitions in dreams. In general, the denizen of the ancient world feels himself surrounded by the supernatural; even among men of education, from the second century of our era on, the belief in the supernatural and the constant recourse to it gains ground at the expense of reason. Thus the religious experience of Aristides must have seemed quite normal to his contemporaries. Many another man could have boasted of divine manifestations in his dreams. But they had not the time to dwell on them. They had to earn their daily bread. The hard labors of the day made them forget the dreams of the night.

VII

Reflective Piety

Man and the World

In the third chapter we saw that, in Plato's last period, that of the *Timaeus* and the *Laws*, his philosophy included a doctrine of the world. The world, or at least the celestial part of it, was thought to constitute an Order, since the heavenly bodies move in regular modes. Since these movements are regular, and since all autonomous motion implies the presence of a soul, it follows that the movements of the heavenly bodies imply the existence of an intelligent World-Soul. Since the human soul, which is likewise intelligent, comes from the heavenly bodies, it is related to them, and its function in the human body is to impose upon the body an order similar to that of the heavens. Finally, since this World-Soul is God, since the World is a god, and since the heavenly bodies are gods, to establish within oneself an order like that of the heavens is to assimilate oneself to God. Thus Plato, ever faithful to the principle of ὁμοίωσις θεῷ—becoming, or being made, like God,—simply enriched this precept here with a new meaning and with moral and spiritual possibilities hitherto unsuspected.

I also stated that this last form of Platonic philosophy played a predominant part in Hellenistic and Greco-Roman times. But it is a remarkable circumstance that, when this doctrine came to have most influence over the souls of men, it was not under the auspices of Plato himself. The Old Academy under Speusippus and Xenocrates devoted most of its energies to the doctrine of Numbers, which seems to have played a large part in the speculations of Plato in his old age. As for the New Academy of Arcesilas and Carneades, it seems to have concerned itself almost entirely with problems of epistemology. But the theory of the World-Soul, with all its implications, became part of Stoicism, and it was under the auspices of the Stoa that the philosophy of the *Timaeus* and the *Laws* first began to exercise its influence on a wide scale.

It is not my task here to mark the technical differences which distinguish Stoicism from Platonism; that is of interest only for specialists. Let me rather present the points of similarity between the two, and show how the fundamental doctrines of the Stoa were such as to create a kind of spirituality and to raise men's souls toward the Cosmic God.

The entire Universe is a great living Whole permeated and vivified by one and the same Fire-Logos. This Fire, a mere principle of cohesion in inanimate things, is, in living beings, also the principle of life at all the levels at which life manifests itself: vegetative in plants, animal in animals, and reasonable in man and in the astral deities. This Life-Soul which penetrates all things, is, as one can see, the same as the Platonic World-Soul, with the difference that whereas Plato left it an open question whether the Soul is immanent in the World or transcendent above it—whence came possible developments in the direction of the transcendental Prime Mover of Aristotle—the Stoics definitely decided for immanence. Now this Fire-Logos is God, so that all beings follow the plan of God. However, there is a great difference between man and all other beings; lesser beings follow God by necessity inasmuch as, being inert or at most provided with instinct alone (which is the situation of animals), they are devoid of intelligence and of conscious will, and therefore are incapable of understanding and inquiring into the plan of God; they obey God by an inevitable inclination, since they obey the laws of their nature. At the other extreme, the astral deities follow God by necessity, inasmuch as, being themselves made of fiery substance, and therefore connatural with the Fire-Logos in its pure essence, they are incapable of resistance to God, since their will and His are one; the heavenly bodies achieve their revolutions by a voluntary movement, and this movement is in eternal conformity with the divine plan. But with man it is different. He is free to understand and accept God's plan; and he is free to reject it. Of course, this rejection by man can be no obstacle to the fulfillment of the decrees of God; the heavens will continue their revolutions, the seasons will continue to come at their appropriate times, the lesser creatures will continue to follow their nature, and even the course of human affairs will unfold itself as it has been foreordained. But man himself will be profoundly unhappy, because he will be fundamentally at variance with his own nature, with the divine Logos which gives him life. Wisdom therefore consists in spontaneous submission to the plan of God, so that one accepts of one's own will that which must in any event come to pass. All Stoic morality can be defined as a "morality of consent." Consent is, after all, the only important thing, and I am among those who believe that the Stoic paradoxes are not paradoxical at all, but actually required by logical necessity, once one has grasped the simple and beautiful doctrine of Zeno. Either one consents, or one rebels; there is no middle ground. If the wise man consents, if he is truly at one with the divine Will, then he is, like God, above all things, beyond the reach of all contingencies, perfectly free, sufficient unto himself. Furthermore, if he is truly at one with God, he cannot do anything wrong. Elsewhere[1] I have compared this Stoic doctrine of consent to the Christian doctrine of love on the highest level, which is in fact its closest analogue. The Stoic sage who lives in harmony with God is no longer capable of sin. St. Augustine says for his part: *Ama et fac quod vis.* "Love, that is, love the will of God, love the plan of God; once you have done that, do as you think fit: whatever you do will be in accordance with God." There is only one reservation to be made, and the Stoic is the first to admit it; that is, that the true sage is a rare being, and it is even a question whether he has ever existed.

You can see immediately the consequences that such a doctrine may have for men's religious attitude. We must go into the problem more deeply.

Let us frankly admit it; it is often difficult to maintain a belief in divine Providence, in a God who loves men and pities them in their misery. That is why the earliest attitude of the Greeks was that the gods are indifferent to the ills of man; that they even take pleasure in them. We can find nothing more melancholy than Greek pessimism; I refer you on this point to the texts collected by Professor Greene of Harvard University.[2] That is also why the Greeks of the Hellenistic Age felt so strongly that all things in this world are ruled by a blind Fortune or by an inexorable Destiny. It is the spontaneous reaction of the man in the street.

The Christian and the Stoic alike reject this attitude of the man in the street, and both alike admit the reality of a divine Providence. It is interesting to see what they have in common and in what points they differ.

What they have in common is the notion, already put forward by Plato, that pessimism usually considers no more than a minute fraction of the whole of reality, and that thus, blinded and confused by the partial disorder affecting its exponents personally, it fails to see the order of the Whole. Salvation then, for the Christian as well as for the Stoic, consists in somehow divesting himself of his merely personal consciousness. We must go beyond our individual selves, forget our personal troubles, and take cognizance of the beauty of the Whole. Having done this, we shall see that what we regarded as disorder and took to be universal, because we made of ourselves the center of the Universe and were interested only in ourselves, in reality leads to a higher Order, loses itself in that Order, and becomes a part of it. Even so the dwellers in a mountain valley ever covered by mist, if they never left that valley, could well believe that the entire earth is a dark and unhappy place; but if they should scale the mountain peaks bordering that valley, they would see the sun making all things bright.

Thus for the Christian and for the Stoic the contemplation of the World-Order requires a sublimation. The problem for the Stoic is to unite the small portion of Logos which he bears within himself to that Logos which animates the universe; then he will understand the plan of God. Once he has understood it, he will be filled with admiration for the eternally wise counsels of heaven, and will praise God. The problem of the Christian is to make his will, set right by Grace, at one with the Will of God; Christian love is a pure and disinterested love by which one finds joy only in that which is pleasant to God and desires only that. It may be that I suffer here on this earth and see suffering all about me; nevertheless, not my will, but Thine, O God, be done.

These things the Stoic and the Christian have in common. Next let us examine the points in which they differ.

The Order at which the Stoic aims is truly the World-Order, and it is a static Order. To leave himself behind, to forget his troubles, the Stoic has only to gaze upon the unvarying movements of the sky and there recognize the perfection of divine Wisdom. The Stoic makes no personal contribution to this celestial Order; it is already there, predestined from eternity to be as it is; and no human effort can effect in it the slightest change whatever. The most the Stoic can do, if he occupies in this world some position of influence, is to attempt to establish in the sublunar sphere a limited and relative order after the pattern of the Order of the Cosmos. Even in this respect, the true Stoic labors under few illusions. Marcus Aurelius does not deceive himself about men any more than he does about the actual results of his administration. In any case, that is not the important thing. The important thing is a man's own pureness of intention. Let the individual will be entirely in accord with God; all the rest, whatever consequences his acts may have, hardly matters. The true Stoic, despite what he may appear to be at first sight, is fundamentally a pure contemplative. He is always looking toward the Whole, and that is enough.

The Order at which the Christian aims is the Order of the city of man, and it is a dynamic Order. It is not given; it must be made. The duty of the Christian is to contribute to its making. The City of the Future cannot be seen; it is as yet entirely hidden in the impenetrable counsels of God. Therefore the

Christian lives of necessity by faith. However, the Christian has this assurance, that all his acts, all his thoughts, all his desires, all the sufferings which he accepts, even his very faults, provided that he redeems them by repentance, work toward the final good: *omnia cooperantur in bonum*. And so the Stoic lacks what the Christian finds indispensable, and this is essentially what distinguishes the two: the virtue of *hope*. Pure Stoic doctrine has no place for hope. Indeed, what could one look forward to, since all things are settled in advance by immutable decree?

To this most important problem of hope I shall return shortly, when I come to speak about Marcus Aurelius. But first we must give some examples of Stoic piety, or, if you will, of Stoic mysticism. It is a mysticism of consent. Man does more than accept God's plan; he admires it and praises it, and finds his happiness in adhering with his whole soul to the working out of this plan.

✧   ✧   ✧

The finest examples of this sort of union with God are to be found in Cleanthes' *Hymn to Zeus* and in the *Meditations* of the emperor Marcus Aurelius.

"Is it not our function," asks Epictetus, "when we dig, when we labor, when we eat, to sing the hymn in praise of God? . . . If I were a nightingale, I should accomplish the task of the nightingale; if I were a swan, I should accomplish the task of the swan. But I am a creature of reason: therefore I must sing the praise of God."[3] To sing the praise of God in all one's acts is the rule of conduct adopted by Cleanthes, the first successor of Zeno. He was still quite young when he left his home in Assos in the Troad for love of wisdom. At Athens he had to earn his living. During the day he attended the lectures of Zeno, and at night he drew and fetched water from a well to irrigate the vegetables of a market gardener. Despite the hardship entailed, this persevering worker succeeded in assimilating not only the subtleties of Greek dialectic but also the fine points of the Greek language. His meter is correct; his style is beautifully simple, without any of the affectations beloved of the semicultured. He was a man of duty. His moral influence was such that the city entrusted him with the education of its youth, and that he was the obvious choice to succeed Zeno as the head of the School. He was also a profoundly religious man. There is an unmistakable tone in the *Hymn to Zeus*.

> Most glorious of immortals, Zeus all powerful, ·
> Author of Nature, named by many names, all hail!
> Thy law rules all . . .
> So will I praise Thee, ever singing of thy might.[4]

The poet goes on to describe the almightiness of God. All the universe obeys him, as a whole and in its parts, the heavens, the earth, the sea. All creatures of necessity follow his law, since they follow their own natures, all save the wicked, and these, being wicked, are fools.

> All things confess Thee . . .
> Save what in foolishness is wrought by evil men.

Yet even this, the faults of the wicked, vanishes into the Order that is the will of Zeus.[5]

> But into harmony thou canst turn such discords
> And make of chaos order; for hate with Thee is love,
> And thus by Thee all things of good and evil are joined
> To make thy eternal Word.

In truth, all these guilty men, who are unable to hear the voice of Zeus and are continually enslaved by their passionate desire for glory, for wealth, or for carnal pleasures, are nothing more than miserable puppets.

> Fools all, who spending folly
> In conflict striving with their own desire of good,
> Hither and thither are borne in the wake of vanity.

There follows the moving conclusion of the hymn: may God have mercy on men, may he deliver them.

> O Zeus that givest all, bear us and bring salvation . . .
> Save men from all their ignorance and its distress.

Then will humanity, possessed once more of wisdom, and constituting a city which is, like the Universe, harmony, give thanks to God for the grace he has shown them:

> So for our meed of honor
> May we requite Thee with the honor of our song,
> And ever praise Thee and thy works.

Let us keep well in mind that this prayer was written three centuries before the Christian era by a pagan who knew nothing of Christ, who had not heard "Our Father who art in heaven," who had not received the proclamation of the Kingdom of God, who lived without the hope of a life after death, who had no other desire than to do on this earth the will of God. How many Christians would be worthy of this pagan?

❖ ❖ ❖

Cleanthes was a humble peasant. On the contrary, Marcus Aurelius was the Emperor of Rome; that is to say, one of the most powerful beings humanity has ever known. From the Euphrates to Britain, from the mouth of the Rhine to the edges of the African desert, his word was law. Yet this autocrat and the humble disciple of Zeno have not a few points of resemblance. Like Cleanthes, Marcus Aurelius was essentially a man of duty. Though he was not a soldier by temperament, it was his destiny to live all too frequently in camp.[6] In civil life, inclined by nature to meditation, to the quiet walks that favor thought and prayer, he was kept by his office in Rome. But he still had a longing for those country villas which wealthy Romans enjoyed in the mountains or on the shores of Campania (IV 3, 1): "They seek retreats for themselves, in the country, on the seashore, in the hills. And you yourself, you too are always yearning after such places."[7] Notwithstanding this, he takes up the burden of his duties, reads the official reports addressed to him, receives the crowd of flatterers whom he de-

spises (II 1, 1), willingly submits to the rules of a court eti-
quette established by his predecessors. The emperor is not his
own master; he is the slave of his rank. And so it is that in this
splendid house on the Palatine where he is served by a multitude
of men, he is in reality more lonely than the lowest of the
Romans. Yet Marcus Aurelius is a man of great sensibility, who
has need of friendship. And so, having no one in whom to con-
fide, and being only too well aware that all those who come near
him with smiles on their lips are smiling only to gain their own
ends, he makes himself his own confidant. It is for this reason
that the *Meditations*, or, to make a more exact translation,
Confidences Made to Myself, Τὰ εἰς ἑαυτόν, is still today one of the
most fascinating books that one can read.

When dealing with a man of such nobility of soul as Marcus
Aurelius, we must not waste words, but look at things as they
are. All life on this earth takes place, as we said before, as if
there were no God, or as if God were indifferent to human suffering. This is the complaint of the young man in the *Laws*.
Plato in his old age and the Stoic would console me by telling
me that I am but a part of the Whole and that this Whole is
well ordered. "We commonly say: 'Asclepius ordered a man to
go horseback riding, to take cold baths, or to walk barefoot.'[8]
Similarly we might say: 'Universal Nature ordered him sickness, disablement, loss, or some other affliction.' In the former
phrase 'ordered' virtually means 'laid this down for him as appropriate to health'; in the latter, 'what befits every man has
been laid down for him as appropriate to the Natural Order.' "
(V 8, 1 ff.) "Welcome," says Marcus Aurelius too (V 8, 10), "all
that comes to pass, even though it appears rather cruel, because
it leads to that end, to the health of the Universe, that is, to the
welfare and well-being of Zeus." And in another place (V 8, 12):
"You must be content with what happens to you . . . because
that which has come to each individually is a cause of the welfare and the completion and in very truth of the actual con-
tinuance of that which governs the Whole."[9]

All that is very beautiful. But I must say *simpliciter* that I don't give a hang for the Natural Order; and if the Natural Order implies that I should be ill, or desperate, I cannot but think that the Natural Order is not order at all, but disorder.

"But," says Marcus, "you may at any time you please retreat into yourself" (IV 3, 2), and there, within yourself, you may find God, touch him (II 12, 4), live with him (V 27, 1). This doctrine of God's indwelling in man is a *Leitmotiv* with Marcus: "Nothing is more wretched than the man who . . . fails to perceive that it is enough to abide with the Divinity that is within himself and to do him genuine service" (II 13, 1). And again: "He is living with the gods who continuously exhibits his soul to them as satisfied with its dispensation and in all things obeying the daimon, this portion of himself which Zeus has given to each man to guard and to guide him" (V 27, 1).[10]

Now who is this god who dwells in me? "This deity—a portion of Zeus in us—is each man's mind and reason."[11] So that, really, it all means that I do not count as myself, as a living being of flesh and blood, with a heart, with personal longings and sorrows, with an ineradicable desire of happiness, but only as I am a part of the Whole. Now the Whole is always well ordered, good, and happy. Therefore, as I am a part of this beautiful Whole, I must consider myself as well treated and happy. And if I am not happy, it is my fault.

We have here, I think, the core of the problem. Suppose that I am ill, in the hospital, quite alone, dying. Not a soul in the world cares for me. I feel that all my life has been a waste, an absolutely nonsensical waste. I know that millions and millions live and die with the same feeling of absurdity, that it has been so since the beginning of the race of men, and will be so till the final consummation. I know that, as a man empowered with reason, I am the only being on earth who can be conscious of these things. I know, then, that all the history of humanity is a farce. And now I ask: If these are the facts, what can really be the meaning of your "Order of the Whole"? What kind of Order can there be when the only reasonable part of that Order cannot but be conscious of a general failure?

You say: "Retreat into yourself and you will find God." But, my dear sir, this God, as you said yourself, is my reason. And my reason is precisely what I hate most of all things, since it is by my reason that I know that all humanity goes wrong, that all human life is nonsense.

Now if this God whom you said I might find within me, if this God were truly another being than myself, and if I could be persuaded that this other being came into myself to be with me, to be my friend, so that I might not live and die quite alone; and moreover, if I could be persuaded that, after this short and painful life, I was to go to this God and remain eternally with him—that would be another matter. In that case, I should have *hope*, I should hope to find, at last, happiness. And after all, when all is said, when all the beautiful and noble phrases about the World's order and the World's happiness are uttered, experience shows that you cannot build human life without taking into account the happiness of man.

The difficulties I have raised here concern, of course, only the doctrine of Marcus Aurelius. They do not detract in the least from his moral greatness.

Marcus Aurelius seems at first sight the most extraordinary figure of all antiquity. He appears to have no illusions about anything. What a terrible reflection is this one (X 36, 1 ff.): "No one is so fortunate but that when he is dying some will be at his bedside welcoming the evil that is coming to him. Was he earnest and wise? Perhaps there will be someone at the end to say of him: 'We shall breathe more freely now that this schoolmaster is gone . . .' So much for the earnest man. But in our own case what a number of other things there are for which many want to be rid of us. You will think of this as you die and will depart more easily, thinking to yourself: 'I am going away from the kind of life in which even my fellow men, for whom I labored, prayed, and thought so much, even they wish me to go away—hoping perhaps for some relief by my death.'"

Yet Marcus' motto throughout his entire life was: "To worship and bless the gods, and to do good to men" (V 33, 6).[12]

Where did he find the courage, each day, to fulfill his human task? and to deprive himself, for this purpose, of all the things he loved most—poetry and liberal studies (I 17, 8), philosophical meditation (I 17, 22), long hours spent in reading (III 14), solitude in some lovely country retreat (IV 3, 1), too often to be exchanged perforce for the unlovely camp?

We must first keep in mind the strength of the Roman tradition, the sense of duty that was so deeply rooted in the minds of the Roman ruling class. "Be a Roman and a man, be a real man, a statesman, a Roman, a chief," the emperor tells himself again and again (II 5, 1; III 5, 2). "Therefore each hour be minded . . . to do what is at hand with precise and unaffected dignity" (II 5, 1: μετὰ τῆς ἀκριβοῦς καὶ ἀπλάστου σεμνότητος). That is the lesson he drew from his adoptive father, Antoninus the Laborious (φιλόπονος) (VI 30, 10), and that lesson was a rule of conduct for him throughout his life. There can be no argument about duty. An emperor naturally finishes "the task he has in hand."[13]

But we must also reflect that Marcus Aurelius was sustained by a living piety which tempers the austerity of his doctrine. In the chapter on what he has received from the gods (I 1), he speaks of divine inspirations: "As far as concerns the gods and communications from the other world, and aids and inspirations . . ." (I 17, 12). He reproaches himself for not having always observed ". . . the reminders and almost the instructions of the gods" (ibid.). He thanks the gods for ". . . having granted him assistance in dreams, especially in the matter of spitting blood and fits of giddiness" (I 17, 20; cf. IX 27, 3). In certain ways, then, Marcus Aurelius is close to his contemporary Aristides. He believed in personal gods who sustained him and consoled him in his troubles. And in one place, at least, he hopes that he will join the gods after death: "As you intend to live when you depart . . ." (V 29, 1).

These features of Marcus Aurelius' religion make him seem closer to us. He is no longer the wise man of utter and inhuman detachment that the pure Stoic seems to us to be. He is, after all, a man like us, who needs consolation, who needs the gods to be near him and to talk with him, who cannot entirely do without the promise of happiness after death.

⟡ ⟡ ⟡

There is another and less austere aspect of the religion of the cosmos which I should like to set forth at the end of this chapter. It is an aspect more aesthetic and less abstract. For the Stoic as for Plato in his old age, not only the World-Soul is divine—it is called Zeus or the Reason of Zeus,[14]—the visible world itself is also god; and the visible heavenly bodies are gods. The ancients never took offense at polytheism; and those of them who concerned themselves with theological problems never considered that the multiplication of divine beings implied any degradation of the Godhead. On the contrary, to the objections of the strictly monotheistic Jews the pagans answered that God is not exalted by being held to be unique; the preëminence of God is made more manifest if he rules over gods of inferior rank than if he is the only god in existence.[15] Therefore there is a divine court; and the heavenly bodies as gods are like the satraps or the bodyguards of God, the Great King, according to the comparison in Philo and the *de Mundo*.[16]

The heavenly bodies are gods. They offer themselves to our eyes with an incomparable splendor. On a clear night in the Near East, or even in Italy, we see them glitter as they form above the city of men another city of divine living beings, possessed of bodies—the bodies that we see shining in the heavens, —but possessed also of souls and of intelligences. Between this city of men and the city of the gods there is a special bond. The Universe, according to the Stoics, is the city inhabited in common by men and by the gods.[17] Now both men and gods participate fully in Logos; both alike are endowed with reason, and hence are able to understand, to admire, and to praise God. But whereas men are troubled by discord in countless forms and by misfortunes without number, the star-gods live always in peace, composing a symphony which no false note ever spoils. To leave our troubles behind, then, we must raise ourselves up by contemplation to the astral deities. So we are back to the old theme of φυγὴ ὁμοίωσις θεῷ, "to flee is to become like God." In this final manifestation the theme comes to be a sort of "astral mysticism," to use the name invented by Franz Cumont.[18]

That the sense of our union with the heavenly bodies could give rise to a profound and sincere form of personal piety is shown by a famous passage in the writings of the emperor Julian: "For I am a follower of King Helios. And of this fact I possess within me, known to myself alone, proofs more certain than I can give. But this at least I am permitted to say without sacrilege, that from my childhood an extraordinary longing for the rays of the god penetrated deep into my soul; and from my earliest years my mind was so completely swayed by the light that illumines the heavens that not only did I desire to gaze intently at the sun, but whenever I walked abroad in the night season, when the firmament was clear and cloudless, I abandoned all else without exception and gave myself to the beauties of the heavens; nor did I understand what anyone might say to me, nor heed what I was doing myself. . . . Let what I have said bear witness to this fact, that the heavenly light shone all about me and that it roused and urged me on to its contemplation."[19]

The epigram of the astronomer Ptolemy is equally well known. I quote it in the beautiful translation of Robert Bridges:

> Mortal though I be, yea ephemeral, if but a moment
> I gaze up to the night's starry domain of heaven,
> Then no longer on earth I stand; I touch the Creator,
> And my lively spirit drinketh immortality.[20]

I could cite other texts, for example, certain prologues of the *Anthologion* of the astrologer Vettius Valens. But they would add nothing to those I have just read, and we should not find in them the same personal note. For we must bear in mind that the praise of the heavens, of the planets, and of their regular movements, become a commonplace under the Empire. We soon tire of this sort of cosmic dithyramb. Nor is it always easy to distinguish between what is no more than a literary cliché and what is the expression of true feeling.

I should like to conclude this chapter with one other observation. No feeling is more common than that of the tranquillity of the night, when all things are at rest on earth, and when the majestic figures of the stars move silently across the heavens. It is only natural, then, that the theme of the beauty of the nocturnal heavens should appear here and there in Greek literature as in the literature of other peoples. But here is an interesting fact. It is that after a certain date this theme, always fundamentally the same, of the contrast between the serenity of the celestial bodies and the helplessness and distress of man, presents certain variations, which bring out the changes that took place in the religious mentality of the Greeks.

Let us first take three examples from the archaic and the classic periods. They have this in common, that they all express the contrast between the peace of the heavens and the anguish of the human heart.

A young woman, perhaps Sappho herself,[21] looks out of the window into the night. She feels lonesome. She looks at the heavens and sings:

> The Moon is gone   Time passes on,
> And the Pleiads set,   And passes, yet
> Midnight is nigh;   Alone I lie.[22]

The night watchman in the *Agamemnon* likewise feels anxiety. He is awaiting the flaming signal from Troy, which is to announce the return of his master. He waits. And to banish sleep, he would like to sing. But

> Think I perchance to sing or troll a tune
> For medicine against sleep, the music soon
> Changes to sighing for the tale untold
> Of this house, not well mastered as of old.[23]

And so, for consolation, he turns to the stars:

> This waste of year-long vigil I have prayed
> The gods for some respite, watching elbow-stayed,
> A sleuthhound's watch, above the Atreidae's hall,

Till well I know you, midnight festival
Of swarming stars, and them that lonely go,
Bearers to man of summer and of snow,
Great lords and shining, throned in heavenly fire.[24]

Finally, what is more tragic than the admirable first prologue of Euripides' *Iphigenia at Aulis?* I will admit that this first anapaestic prologue (1–48) is not in harmony with the second prologue (49–109), which is in iambics,[25] but, for my part, I am quite ready to say, with Professor Ed. Fraenkel,[26] that this anapaestic prologue is the genuine work of Euripides, not the dull trimeters of the second. In any case, these lines are the work of a real dramatist and a real poet. Agamemnon is tormented by anguish. Should he send for his daughter Iphigenia from Argos in order to sacrifice her? Or should he countermand the order? In this uncertainty he goes forth from his tent to the beach of Aulis, and suddenly he feels himself filled with the tremendous peace of the night:

What is yonder, traveling in the sky, this brilliant star,
Close to the sevenfold voyaging Pleiades,
Still high overhead?
No sounds from the birds;
No sound from the sea.
The hush of the winds
Broods over Euripus.[27]

Clearly, the feeling in these three texts is the same. The more man is penetrated by his own sorrow, the more vividly he feels the contrast between his own agony and the imperturbable tranquillity of the night sky. But nothing urges him to look to the skies for help; he has no thought of being united to the stars by some part of himself; the idea of seeking refuge with the stars is totally foreign to him.

How different is the mood of Ptolemy and of Julian, and of that revealed in the famous *Nachtlied* of Goethe:

Der du von dem Himmel bist,
Alles Leid und Schmerzen stillest,
Den, der doppelt elend ist,
Doppelt mit Erquickung füllest,

Ach ich bin des Treibens müde!
Was soll all der Schmerz und Lust?
Süsser Friede,
Komm, ach komm in meine Brust![28]

Here, too, man is conscious of his misery. Θνατὸς καὶ ἐφάμερος, says Ptolemy, mortal and ephemeral, and by these two words he expresses everything: man who is of mortal state, and hence destined to all the ills of the mortal state; man, who flits across the earth like the butterfly whose life is but a day. But this man whose life is but for a day feels himself related to the divine stars, bound up in friendship with God himself, capable, whenever he so wishes, of entering again by his thought into the divine city. "No longer on earth he stands." There is a spark within him of that fire which is the substance of the stars themselves. We are familiar with these doctrines, as those of Plato's *Timaeus*. It can be said that they brought about a revolution in the religious sensibility of the West.[29]

VIII

Reflective Piety

The Contemplation of God

IN THE last chapter, we read a page from the emperor Julian, in which, harking back to childhood memories, he tells how he had very early become enthralled by the beauty of the nocturnal sky. Now let us see what another adolescent, a very poor Slavic peasant, born in 1875, who later became a monk, priest, and missionary in Siberia,[1] has to say on that same subject. The experience of this Russian child is extraordinarily like that of the youthful Julian.

"Very early I felt in myself an inclination toward solitary contemplation of God and nature. . . . I was scarcely five years old when I began to flee from my companions and other children of my age in order to go into the forest, to wander over the countryside, to seat myself on knolls in the fields, where I spent hours in meditation. . . . I shall never forget the feeling of joy and ecstasy with which I gazed upon the sun or the milky way. . . . There were nights when everything around me was plunged in deep slumber, and I alone watched, steeping myself to the point of tears in the beauty and harmony of the heavenly bodies. But what astonished me most was that from my earliest childhood I was always aware within myself of a strong inclination toward prayer. In vain did nature charm me with her beauty, in vain did she fill my heart and mind with devotion toward herself—I always felt that that did not suffice, that there was still a place in my soul that prayer alone could fill . . . , not the prayer of churches, not formulas learned by heart, but solitary, childlike prayer, which links the faithful to God."

I have quoted this passage for two reasons. First, because it expresses with perfect clarity the human data, the natural conditions, which the exercise of contemplation supposes in a man; Plato himself had established in the *Republic* (V 475B ff.) that there are beings with a natural bent toward philosophy, that is, are by their very nature in love with wisdom. Secondly, because it shows us already, in summary fashion, the substance of contemplation. It is an ascent which, from the spectacle of visible beauty, causes us to attain to invisible beauty. This passage from the visible to the invisible is essential; it is inherent in the very notion of contemplation. Let us reread the curious lines in which the Russian child naïvely describes his inward impulse, without as yet any very clear understanding of what he feels: "What astonished me most was that from my earliest childhood I was always aware of a strong inclination toward prayer within myself. In vain did nature charm me with her beauty, in vain did she fill my heart and mind with devotion toward herself. I always felt that that did not suffice, that there was still a place in my soul that prayer alone could fill." And the child specifies: not official prayer, which is expressed in formulae learned by heart, but "solitary childlike prayer, which links the faithful to God." In a word, the last stage of the contemplative soul in its flight is total union with God.

It is this phenomenon, such as it manifests itself from the second century of our era onward, that I should like to study in this chapter.

THE SYSTEMATIC FRAMEWORK OF THE ASCENT TOWARD GOD

Once the natural data are granted—by that I mean the contemplative temperament and the practical conditions indispensable to the mystical life: solitude, detachment from the goods of this world (what the Gospel calls poverty of spirit), the practice of withdrawal and inward concentration,—it is clear that the contemplative ascent fits into a certain frame of thought, into an intellectual system wherein the relationships between man, the world, and God are clearly defined. A Russian Orthodox child, in the latter half of the nineteenth century, was definitely inside the framework of the Christian system. Let us inquire what was the frame of thought for a pagan under the Empire from the second to the sixth centuries.

This framework has two levels. It includes an outlook on the physical world, and a perspective on the intelligible world.

The physical world is divided into two parts: the sublunary and the superlunary. The sublunary part consists of the earth upon which we dwell, with the water which covers vast portions of it, then the air of the atmosphere, and finally, fire. On the boundary line of the fiery region we reach the moon, the first and lowest of the planets. These last are composed of a fifth essence, aether, purer than the four sublunary elements. The main difference between the sublunary part of the physical world and the superlunary part is that the latter moves in eternally regular movements whereas all motion in the sublunary part is irregular and disorderly. Then come, above the moon, the six other planets, in the following order: Mercury, Venus, the Sun, Mars, Jupiter, and Saturn. Then the eighth circle or sphere, that of the fixed stars. With this eighth circle ends the physical world.

Every region of this physical world is inhabited by living beings. Earth, water, and air have for inhabitants all the species of animals, including man. The upper air and fire are inhabited by demons and by the souls of the dead who have not yet attained to the superlunary zone. The planetary orbits have for inhabitants the planets; these are themselves living beings, since they are in eternal motion, and living beings endowed with divine intelligence, since their movements are ordained for all eternity. Finally, the supreme God is enthroned above the heaven of the fixed stars, and it is from there on high that he governs the whole universe, the planetary gods, and the demons serving as intermediaries.

This concept of the physical world is founded, as you see, upon a dichotomy which involves a kind of dualism: the dualism of the superlunary part, inhabited by divine beings of ever-regular movements, and of the sublunary part, inhabited by mortal beings of movements not regularly ordered. Moreover,

we already find in this concept an elementary notion of transcendence, crude as yet, and purely physical; the supreme God,
who is enthroned beyond the heaven of the fixed stars, transcends the whole universe.

However, upon this dualism inherent in the physical world,
and upon this early form of transcendence which remains on a
physical plane, is superimposed another kind of dualism and of
transcendence. It is the old Platonic dualism of the sensible
world of becoming and the intelligible world of being. The
physical world, even in its superlunary part, so beautiful, so
well regulated, and already divine, remains nevertheless material, an object which presents itself to our senses. Furthermore, even though the movements of the heavenly world are
regular and intelligent, they remain movements. There subsists, then, something inferior even in the nature of the heavenly
gods; they have a body, and they change. And lastly, the
transcendent God himself, so far as he is conceived as enthroned
physically above the sphere of the fixed stars, is still an element
of this physical system; he no doubt occupies the highest
place—he is called *Deus summus, exsuperantissimus,*—but he is
still a part of the world. With the notion of the intelligible world
we reach a fundamental division—on the one hand, there is
everything which is material, an object of sensory perception,
and on the other, there is everything immaterial, apprehended
by the intellect alone; in a word, Plato's world of Ideas.

However, between the ideal world of Plato himself and that
of the Platonists under the Empire, there is an important difference, and one which is extremely significant for the progress of
the spiritual life. The Ideas of Plato are not the thoughts of
God. They remain exterior to the mind of God. God contemplates them from without, as we ourselves do. Unquestionably,
he contemplates them better, because he is, in a manner of
speaking, very close to them, and because his intellective faculty
is infinitely better than ours.[2] Nevertheless they remain, for him
as for us, extrinsic and superior objects, a pattern for God himself to follow. Therein lies the source of endless difficulties in

original Platonic theology. The Platonists of the Empire, for their part, take the Ideas to be the thoughts of God. "In its relation to God," says Albinus, author of a second-century manual on Platonism, "the Idea is his thought,"[3] as, elsewhere: "The Ideas are the thoughts of God, eternal and perfect in themselves (αὐτοτελεῖς)." The same philosopher demonstrates in the following manner the existence of the Ideas (this is his first argument): "Whether God is an Intellect, or a being possessed of an intellect, he has thoughts, and those thoughts are eternal and immutable. In that case, the Ideas exist."[4] The Ideas are therefore contained in God, and the whole intelligible world thus becomes nothing other than the substance and person of God himself. It is at once apparent how favorable such a doctrine could be to the development of spiritual life. To unite oneself with God, according to Plato's system, one was not really sure whether to seek oneness with the Intelligence which guides the heavenly bodies—such, apparently is the answer given in the *Timaeus*,—or with the supreme Idea situated at the summit of the intelligible world, which is called the Beautiful (*Symposium*), the Good (*Republic*), or the One (*Philebus*). Furthermore, the ascent toward the supreme Idea was only to be made, according to Plato, by means of the purely intellectual exercise of dialectic, and required a long cycle of rational studies in which mathematics played a large role; there was no longer much room for a purely spiritual impetus, for intimacy with God. But henceforth, as soon as one transcends the physical world, one enters into God; one becomes a divine thought, or, as one Hermetic author puts it, one is changed into the (divine) Essence (*Corp. Herm.* X 6, 116.1–2 N.-F.).

But we must be more specific. In this system, God is essentially an intelligence. He has thoughts which are the Platonic Ideas; that is, the exemplary causes of the sensible world. In other words, the entire intelligible world, which is the model of the sensible world, is eternally contained in the divine intellect. But is God *only* an intellect?

In Plato's system, the Ideas constitute a hierarchy, extending

from the Ideas of lowest species, which are closest to the concrete individual, through the most generic Ideas, which include
the greatest number of species, and ending with the primary
genera, that is, with the predications which can be made of any
being in so far as it exists, the Beautiful, the Good, and the One.
But it happened that, once one had arrived at these primary
categories, the denominations of Good, Beautiful, and One
proved inadequate. In point of fact, we had no sooner arrived
at the primal qualities than we found ourselves in the presence
of indefinable and unnamable entities. Plato expresses this with
the greatest clarity in a famous passage of the *Symposium* (210E
ff.). When he comes to define the final term of the ascent to the
Beautiful, he no longer finds any positive signs, but only negative ones; he does not say what the Beautiful is, but only what
it is not: "Whoever has been thus far instructed in the things
of love, and is able to contemplate all beautiful things in due
succession, will suddenly descry, as he comes at last to the end,
a thing in its nature of most wondrous beauty, the very thing,
O Socrates, that was the reason of all our previous labors.
First, it exists eternally, neither coming into being nor passing
away from it; and then it is not beautiful in one way and ugly
in another, or beautiful at one time and not at another, or in
relation to one thing beautiful and not to another, nor yet
beautiful in one place and ugly in another; nor will its beauty
appear to be a human face, or arms, or any other of the parts
of the body, nor any speech or knowledge, nor anything that
might exist in something else, as in a living thing on the earth
or in the heavens or in anything else. Itself by itself with itself,
of one form, it is forever."[5] I have elsewhere[6] put forward the
thesis that an object of which there can be no representation,
either imaginative or intellectual, an object above or beyond
any possible definition or any possible cognition, is an object
above and beyond essence, an *epekeina tes ousias* as it is called
in the *Republic* (VI 509B 8–9). I based upon this exegesis my
opinion that Platonic metaphysics ends in a form of mysticism.
I still believe this opinion to be the correct one; and in any case

it is in this way that the Platonists of the Empire understood Plato. In the second century after Christ, Albinus writes,[7] when he comes to the problem of God: "We have now to speak of the Third Principle;[8] Plato seems almost to consider this as *ineffable* (ἄρρητον)." And later: "The Primal God is eternal, *ineffable* (ἄρρητος)."[9] Later still, in a passage especially reminiscent of the negative method of the *Symposium*: "God, as I have said, is *ineffable* (ἄρρητος), and can be apprehended only by the *nous*."[10] Here we must transcribe the Greek word *nous* and not translate it "intellect," as I have suggested in the third chapter; for *nous*, in Plato and the Platonists, is not only the faculty of intellectual perception by which we apprehend a definite essence, but also the faculty of mystical intuition by which we enter into contact with the Being who is beyond essence. "God is ineffable," says Albinus, "for he is neither genus nor species nor any other specific difference, nor does he admit of any accidental quality; he is neither a bad thing (it would be impiety to say so); nor a good thing (if he were, he would exist by participation in something else, namely, goodness); nor an indifferent thing[11] (for that also could not enter into the notion of God); he is not a thing of this or that quality (for he is not a qualified thing rendered this or that by some quality), nor is he a thing deprived of quality[12] (for he was not denied qualification as though it became him to be qualified); he neither is part of any other thing nor contains parts like a whole; nor is he of such nature as to be identical with any other thing or to be different from any other thing (for he does not admit of any accidental quality by which he might be distinguished from other things); he neither moves other things, nor is himself moved." If God thus escapes every category of language and of thought, it is because in reality he transcends them all. No definition can contain him, because he can be limited by no essence.

Thus we arrive at the notion of a supreme God who is unknowable, *Theos agnostos*. Not entirely unknowable; if we had no idea whatsoever of Him, we should not even know that He exists, and therefore we could never even think of uniting ourselves to Him; but he is rationally, intellectually unknowable, in the sense that no process of thought permits us to come close to Him and that to attain Him therefore we must make use of a superintellectual method. For lack of a better name, this superintellectual knowledge is often called "silence" by the pagan mystics of Imperial times. God is He "of whom no words can tell, no tongue can speak, whom silence only can declare."[13] "Then only will you see it (the beauty of the Good) when you cannot speak of it, for the knowledge of it is divine silence, and suppression of all the senses."[14]

We can now describe, in résumé, the system which serves as a theoretical basis for the ascent toward God. In the lower region, there is the physical world, divided into two parts, the sublunary and the superlunary. Above this, there is the intelligible world, which is also divided into two parts. First, there are the Ideas corresponding to definite essences; they constitute a kind of intelligible double of the sensible world, and are the models, the exemplary causes of this sensible world. Since these Ideas are the thoughts of the Divine Intellect, they, in their hierarchic ensemble, constitute the structure of that Intellect. Since, further, this divine Intellect or primal Intellect, being supremely beautiful, must have as its object of thought something of supreme beauty, and since there can be no object more beautiful than itself, it can only think itself. Thus God thinks the world at the same time that he thinks Himself.[15] The intelligible world as the thought of God and God as Thought which thinks itself are but two related aspects of one and the same reality. But the Ideas in their turn, the thoughts of God, end in a primal Idea, or, if you will, in an Essence which bursts all the limits of Essence, and therefore all the limits of Thought. God himself, in that which constitutes his fundamental Being, can neither know Himself nor express Himself. He is the Unknowable, the Unexpressible. This is that utterly supreme cause which is at the summit of the whole hierarchy. This is, absolutely, the transcendent God.

We have finally arrived at the famous theory of the three

Gods which played a great part in spiritual life from the second century on. From the consideration of the sensible world, at least in its celestial part, one infers the existence of an Intelligent Soul which moves the heavens in eternal and regular movements; it is to this God that the pseudo-Aristotelian *De Mundo* attains. This God of the physical world depends on the Thought which thinks itself, whose thoughts are the Ideas of the intelligible world. Finally, this Intelligible Intellect is itself in dependence on the primal Cause, which is beyond essence, and therefore beyond all intellectual apprehension, truly unknowable, undefinable, unnamable.

This theory of the three Gods was made known most of all by Plotinus with his system of the three hypostases derived one from the other: the One, the Intellect, the World-Soul. But we find it before Plotinus in Numenius and in the Chaldaic Oracles, and it exists in germ in Albinus. After Plotinus, it acquires the standing of a dogma in Porphyry, Iamblichus, and Proclus, and it penetrates far into the Middle Ages.

The doctrine becomes ever more complicated in Plotinus' successors; each of the two inferior hypostases is now conceived as containing a multiplicity of divine component parts. Thus God the World-Soul is subdivided into the planetary gods, who, as souls, are the movers of the planets. God the Intelligible Intellect is divided into two worlds, themselves composed of manifold gods. Since this Intellect is a thinking Thought, each of its thoughts constitutes an intelligent god (νοερός); since the thoughts of this Intellect are the Ideas of the intelligible world, each Idea constitutes in its turn an intelligible god (νοητός); and each of the intelligent gods corresponds to one of the intelligible gods. The only one who remains uncompounded and unique is the primal Cause, the ineffable God.

We can afford to pass over here these complications which have never been of any profit to the spiritual life. On the other hand, I must point out one doctrinal notion which has had great influence on the attitude of religious souls.

Despite its twofold dualism, the system which I have thus far

outlined remains essentially optimistic. In this system, the physical world is truly evil only in its sublunary portion, which is
composed of matter without order and purity. The superlunary
part of this world, being formed of a subtile and pure matter,
the aether, and having regular motion, is good, even divine—the
heavenly bodies are gods. Better yet; even in its sublunary part
the physical world in some fashion participates in the perfection
of the intelligible world, since there is no existent being which
has not within itself, to a greater or smaller extent, the mark of
the Good, the Beautiful, and the One. Thus one can elevate
oneself by a natural progression from the entities of the physical
world to those of the intelligible world, from thence to the Supreme Genera, and from thence to God. God is omnipresent; the
world is filled with Him; it is possible to seek the imprints which
he has set in things, even beginning with the lowest of existing
things. Thus from Plotinus to St. Bonaventure, there exists
an *itinerarium mentis ad deum*. It can be said that this itinerary
reconciles the two currents of Platonic thought, that of the
Timaeus, and that of the great dualistic dialogues, the *Phaedo*,
the *Symposium*, and the *Republic*.

But on the other hand, by emphasizing the dualistic opposition of the *Phaedo* between the sensible and the intelligible, and
by interpreting in a pessimistic sense the concept of matter in
the *Timaeus*,[16] certain thinkers of the Empire came to consider
the entire world evil, since, even in its superlunary part, it is
still made of matter. Matter is the Evil, and all that is material
is *ipso facto* tainted with evil. Therefore not only is it impossible
to find here below any trace of God, but God must be entirely
separated from the world. God and the material world become
two antithetical poles.

But, in that case, how are we to explain the world? It clearly
cannot have come forth from the Primal God, not even by a
series of progressively inferior emanations; the Good can in no
way be the cause of Evil. So the world must be the work of a
Secondary God. But this Secondary God himself, if he is good,
could only have created the world (in the Greek sense of

δημιουργός, Ordainer, not Creator *ex nihilo*) by some kind of error or accident; or, if he did create it of his own free will, this Secondary God must be considered evil, and becomes opposed to the Primal God as an antigod. Certain Gnostics did go this far; and scholars have claimed to find the expression of this doctrine even in such a work as the Hermetic *Poimandres*. Whatever may be said of the system, it is important here to note its consequences for spiritual life. If the world is entirely evil, it not only does not lead to God, but takes one farther from Him. So every representation accessible to the senses must be abolished; nay, all human knowledge must be done away with. For even in man (the highest of the animals), the rational soul is still bound up with the body and dependent on matter. All the processes of the reason help one not one whit to make the ascent toward God. "Those who failed to hear the Divine Proclamation," says one of the Hermetic writers,[17] "are those who possess the *logos* only, but have not received also the *nous*," that is, the faculty of mystical intuition; ". . . these men know not for what purpose they have been made, and by whom they have been made." The entire spiritual quest therefore will consist in gathering together one's faculties within oneself, in ridding oneself of all images and all thoughts, in living in a state of pure passivity in which one hopes, in the end, to find God.

We have seen how God and the world fit into the system. There remains man. The doctrine here is exceedingly simple, the direct consequence of the dualist position. Man is of two substances, matter and *nous*. Matter includes not only the part of man that is the body, but also all that enters into direct relation with the body: the vital soul which animates him, and the temperament which is the result of the mixture of the corporal elements—all that we should today call the individual self. Reason itself, although it is by definition what distinguishes us from the irrational beasts (ἄλογοι), is held by certain Hermetic treatises to be still too much bound up with the material body to be an emanation from above. We have therefore within us only one truly divine element, the *nous*, in its twofold function of intellective faculty and mystical faculty. This dualist view sets the pattern for all human conduct. If matter is Evil, and if the *nous* is the only divine part of man, any ascent toward God reduces itself to two rules; one must withdraw from matter and exercise only the *nous*. But each of these two rules admits of alternative interpretations. To withdraw from matter could mean that one should live a completely ascetic life, like that of the Christian monk; it could also mean that one should let the body do as it pleases, since it after all does not count. A moral code of utmost austerity and another quite easygoing can both be inferred from this principle. On the other hand, the exercise of the *nous* depends on what is meant by *nous*. If *nous* is taken in its twofold meaning as both intellective faculty and mystical faculty, there will result a philosophical contemplation leading, in its final stage, to mystical contact; here we have the true Platonic tradition, that adopted, for example, by Plotinus. If *nous* is taken to mean only the mystical faculty, then one must mistrust all intellectual activity, even the most lofty, and devote oneself entirely to prayer. Such is the tendency given expression in several Hermetic treatises. "Philosophy," says the *Asclepius* (12 ff.), "is nothing else than striving through constant contemplation and saintly piety to attain to knowledge of God, but there will be many who will corrupt philosophy itself with manifold speculations." How so? asks the disciple. Hermes answers: "In this way, Asclepius: by a cunning sort of invention, in which philosophy will be mixed with diverse and unintelligible sciences, such as arithmetic, music, and geometry." Now, proceeds Hermes, all these sciences are absolutely futile. They can be good only when they lead to God; for example, when, seeing the order and beauty of the cosmos, you revere, adore, and praise God's skill and wisdom. This is the conclusion (14): "I tell you then that the men of after times will be misled by cunning sophists, and will be turned away from true, pure, and holy philosophy. For to worship the Godhead in thought and spirit with singleness of heart, to revere God in all His works, and to give thanks to God's will . . . , this is philosophy unsullied by intrusive cravings for unprofitable knowledge." In a word, "piety is the knowledge of God."[18] This is the motto of Hermetism.

THE STAGES OF THE ASCENT TOWARD GOD

Now that the framework has been established, we are in a position to describe the stages of the mystical journey. One point is clear at the outset. The various forms of mysticism under the Empire will be defined by the stage at which one stops in the ascent. There will be contemplation of the Cosmic God, or of the world throughout all of which God penetrates. There will be contemplation of the intelligible world which, as we have seen, is at the same time the Thought of the Second Intellect-God, or this Intellect-God considered as the Thinking Thought. And finally there will be, beyond all thought, an exceedingly mysterious union with the ineffable Primal God.

You have already been provided, in the preceding chapter, with some texts concerned with the aesthetic contemplation of the celestial world. It goes without saying that this aesthetic contemplation can straightway turn into religious contemplation since the vision of the cosmic order leads to the thought of the ordering God. This theme has given rise to countless developments, of which some appear to be no more than mere literary exercises (such as we find so often in Cicero and in Philo of Alexandria), whereas others may have had some religious value. Here is a single example from the *Corpus Hermeticum* (V 3-5): "If you wish to see Him (God), observe the Sun, observe the course of the Moon, observe the order of the stars. Who is it that maintains that order? . . . Someone there must be, my son, who is the maker and master of all these. . . . Would that it were possible for you to grow wings, and to soar into the air! Poised between earth and heaven, you might see the solid earth, the fluid sea and the streaming rivers, the freely moving air, the penetrating fire, the courses of the stars, the swiftness of the heaven, its ceaseless motion round the poles. What happiness were that, my son, to see in one moment all these marvels, and to behold the Unmoved moving, the Hidden one manifesting Himself in His works."

One more rung up the ladder, and we have attained to the Intellect-God who contains within himself, as his Thoughts, all the Ideas of the intelligible world, and therewith, since these Ideas are the eternal models of sensible things, the entire sensible world as well. To attain to this God, who is at one and the same time the Thinking Intellect and the intelligible world as conceived by the divine Thought, we are no longer guided by the objects of the senses. We must with one leap go beyond all that is accessible to the senses and pass into the unknown. This requires an immense effort, which is described in the fourth Hermetic treatise (8–9): "You see, my son, through how many bodily things we have to make our way, and through how many troops of daimones and planetary spheres in succession, and courses of stars, that we may press on to the one and only God. For we can never reach the farther boundary of the Good; it is limitless and without end. . . . Let us then . . . make our way thither with all speed. It is in truth a tortuous way, since we have to forsake the familiar things around us, and turn back to the old home whence we came. Things seen delight us, and things unseen give rise to disbelief. Now the things that are evil are more manifest to sight; but the Good cannot be seen by things manifest; for it has no form or shape." Despite these difficulties, if we arm ourselves with courage and make once and for all the required effort, we can reach a sort of ecstasy in which, lost in the divine Intellect, we lose ourselves also in the totality of His thought, that is, in the whole universe that He contains in His thought. A strange passage of the eleventh treatise thus recommends self-transcendence and union with Aion, who plays here the part of Second God, intermediary between the Supreme God and the world. The author has just demonstrated that, if we are capable by our thought of extending ourselves everywhere, even to the heavens, the divine Thought is *a fortiori* capable of embracing the universe. "You must understand, then, that this is how God contains within himself the Cosmos, and himself, and all that is; it is as thoughts which God thinks, that all things are contained in him" (XI 20). Then, without any transition, one comes to a sermon on ecstasy: "If then you do not make yourself equal to God, you cannot apprehend God; for like is known by like. Make yourself grow to a like expanse with that greatness which is beyond all measure, leap clear of all that is corporeal, rise above all time and become Aion; then you will apprehend God. Think that for you too nothing is impossible; deem that you too are immortal, and that you are able to group all things in your thought, to know every craft, every science, the temper of every living creature; make yourself higher than all heights, and lower than all depths; bring together in yourself the sensations of all created things, of fire and water, of dry and wet; think that you are everywhere at once, on land, at sea, in heaven, that you are not yet begotten, that you are in the womb, that you are young, that you are old, that you have died, that you are beyond the grave, grasp in your thought all these things at once, all times and places, all substances and qualities and magnitudes together; then you can apprehend God." One may doubt whether there is here any real spiritual experience, and suspect that it is rather a piece of rhetorical emphasis expressing only the simple truth that the range of human thought is infinite. But a parallel passage proves that whatever the reality may be, the Hermetist here seeks to describe an inward and personal experience. In the thirteenth treatise of the *Corpus Hermeticum*, which deals with spiritual regeneration, the newly regenerated disciple expresses his own feelings. He has just undergone a "revival." He has put on the new man, in the form of divine Powers, and cast off the old. Here is how he describes his "rebirth" (XIII 11): "I was made immovable by the grace of God, Father, and I perceive things now, not with bodily eyesight, but with the mystical faculty which the Powers have given to me! I am in heaven and on earth, in water and in air; I am in beasts and plants; I am a babe in the womb, and one that is not yet conceived, and one that has been born; I am present everywhere." Clearly, what this mystic would express is an experience in which he has so thoroughly gone beyond himself that he bursts all limits of space and time, makes himself equal to the infinity and eternity of the total Intellect, and becomes himself the intelligible Intellect.

One more rung up the ladder, and we have attained to the object to which Plato had already given the name of "the vast sea of beauty,"[19] and which, as a Hermetic treatise describes it (XIII 6), is that which "is not sullied [by matter], nor limited by boundaries, that which has no color and no shape and is not subject to change, that which is without integument, and is luminous, that which is apprehended by itself alone, the unalterable Good, the Incorporeal." Noteworthy in this passage is the alternation of positive and negative terms. Of the negative terms, some are applicable to all that is incorporeal—"that which is not sullied [by matter], that which has no color and shape and is not subject to change . . ."; others apply only to the primal Incorporeal—"that which is not limited by boundaries and is apprehended by itself alone," that is to say: "is not apprehended by us, is in itself incomprehensible." The positive terms are either traditional expressions going back to Plato himself—"the unalterable Good"—or else a metaphor taken from light: "that which is shining, luminous." This variety of terms manifests the difficulty inherent in the description of an object which, properly speaking, cannot be described. What possibly remains the best inadequate designation of it is the image of light, so dear to Hellenistic mysticism.[20] In a later time, frequent reference will be made to the Divine Darkness; for this light which is God is of such brightness that it blinds us. Bultmann holds that this image of the divine Obscurity does not appear before Pseudo-Dionysus the Areopagite, around 500 A.D.[21] Yet one feels at least the beginning of it in Philo[22] in a passage where he alludes to the luminous cloud in Exodus (20: 21): "So Moses," he says, "this man who contemplated the Being without form—for the divine oracles tell us that he entered into the *cloud*, by which they wish to signify the invisible and incorporeal Essence . . ." It may be that this idea reappears in a Hermetic treatise, if we accept a plausible correction by Ferguson and Cumont.[23] If so, we get this sense: "Father, you have given me my fill of this good and most beautiful sight; and my mind's eye is almost blinded by the splendor of the vision." Nay, answers Hermes, the Divine Light is not a thing of fire, like the rays of the sun. "It does not blaze down upon us and force us to close our eyes. . . . It is, indeed, more penetrating than visible light, but it is not harmful." You can see how close we are here, perhaps, to the idea of the Divine Darkness. Hermes' very denial proves that certain minds had already conceived the notion. Besides, in many other passages Philo speaks of the dizziness which overtakes us when we approach God. But dizziness in Greek is σκοτοδινία, which means a whirling in the darkness.

Another image used to designate the Supreme God is that of the solitude in which God dwells, enjoying eternal rest. We come across this image in a beautiful fragment of Numenius:[24] "It is possible," he says, "for us to understand corporeal things. We recognize them by their resemblance to other things of the same kind and by the signs which they offer to our senses. But there is no way of understanding the Good, neither by any sign offered to our senses, nor by any sensible object bearing a resemblance to it. This is what one must do. It is as if one were standing on a high point of vantage and looking out into the far distance at one of those tiny barks in which men go fishing.[25] It is isolated and alone, lost in the desert of the waters, cradled in the hollow of the waves. But if one looks very hard, one will see it—for an instant. So it is with the Good. One must go far away from sensible things and converse alone with the Good alone, in a place where there is neither human creature, nor any other living thing, nor any corporeal thing great or small, but only an ineffable, inexpressible, incredibly wonderful solitude. There it is that the Good dwells in all its splendor. He himself is there, in tranquillity, in joyous mood, he the Calm, the Sovereign Guide; there he smiles, borne on the chariot of Essence."

It is with this text of such wondrous beauty that I should like to end this chapter, and the book as well.

"To converse alone with God alone" (ὁμιλῆσαι μόνῳ μόνον). This expression, to be found in some Platonists of the Empire, Numenius and Plotinus for example,[26] sums up admirably all that I have tried to tell you. I have tried to show you that there was, throughout the history of Greek religion, from at least the time of Heraclitus and the tragedians, a desire to enter into direct, intimate, and personal contact with the divinity. The concept of God may have changed; the desire to see God, to touch Him, to talk with Him, heart to heart, did not change. The chorus of the *Agamemnon* addresses its anxious prayer to a Zeus who is already an ineffable God, whose real name no one knows, and who can be compared only with Himself (*Agam.* 160–165). Hippolytus forsakes his comrades to pray tenderly to his goddess. According to Plato, the summit of human experience is the ineffable contact by which we are united to the highest Reality. The hero of Apuleius finds happiness in the loving contemplation of Isis. The Hermetist lives, or tries to live, in the constant sense of the presence of God. "Everywhere God will come to meet you, everywhere He will appear to you, at places and times at which you look not for it, in your waking hours and in your sleep, when you are journeying by water and by land, in the nighttime and in the daytime, when you are speaking and when you are silent" (*Corp. Herm.* XI 21).

And so this great and noble literature of Greece reminds us unceasingly that, to use the expression of Plato (*Tim.* 90A 5, BC), the best part of us lifts us up from earth toward our celestial affinity, like a plant whose roots are not in earth, but in the heavens. "Now," says he, "if the heart of man has been set on the love of learning and true wisdom and he has exercised that part of himself above all, he is surely bound to have thoughts immortal and divine, if he shall lay hold upon truth, nor can he fail to possess immortality in the fullest measure that human nature admits; and because he is always devoutly cherishing the divine part and maintaining the guardian genius that dwells with him in good estate, he must needs be happy above all."[27]

Notes

NOTES TO CHAPTER I

The Two Currents in Personal Religion
Popular Piety: Hippolytus and Artemis
(Pages 1–18)

1 This is at least what one feels when reading some of the old Attic dedications to Athena, as, for example, No. 37 in P. Friedländer and H. B. Hoffleit, *Epigrammata* (Univ. of California Press, 1948), with the charming ending ᾧ (ἄγαλμα) χαίρουσα διδοίης ἄλλο ἀναθεῖναι, which adds, it seems, some sort of arch playfulness and gentle intimacy to the usual formulae: δὸς χαρίεσσαν ἀμοιβάν (Nos. 35 and 36), or ὧν χάριν ἀντιδίδου (No. 106a, b), or τῶν ἀγαθῶν τῷ σὺ δὸς ἀφθονίαν (No. 147). Now of course the existence of this document (No. 37) and the lack of such documents for the other gods honored at Athens may be only a matter of chance. However, we should note with V. Ehrenberg, *The People of Aristophanes*, 2d ed. (Oxford, 1951) 264, that Athena, with the two Eleusinian goddesses, is always in Old Comedy "safe from being exposed to comic indecency and coarse ribaldry." Besides, with regard to the other Olympians at Athens, we have nothing similar to the stele of Athena mourning for the dead. After all, Athena is ἡ πολιοῦχος, the guardian goddess of the sacred land of Attica, ἡ τῆς ἱερωτάτης μεδέουσα χώρας of Ar. *Eq.* 581 ff. In the *Septem* of Aeschylus the πολισσοῦχοι or πολιοῦχοι θεοί come first in the prayers of Eteocles (69 [here with Zeus and Ge], 271) and of the Chorus (312, 322 [here with Zeus]).

2 Werner Jaeger, *The Theology of the Early Greek Philosophers* (Oxford, 1947).

3 "Zeus ist nicht mehr ein Gott, wenn auch der mächtigste, wie bei Homer, sondern ist Gott, . . . der Schirmherr der Gerechtigkeit, der von uns einen gerechten Wandel verlangt, und unerbittlich die strafende Gerechtigkeit ausübt." Wilamowitz, *Hesiod: Erga* (Berlin, 1928) 158. Cf. Pindar, *Isthm.* V, and Wilamowitz, *Pindaros* (Berlin, 1922) 205.

4 Cf. note 1 *supra*.

5 Aristotle, fr. 15 Rose. Cf. J. Croissant, *Aristote et les mystères* (Liège, 1932) 137 ff.

6 Plato, *Phaedo* 69D 1.

143

[7] Aristophanes, *Ranae* 886 f. The translation is Gilbert Murray's, in his edition of *The Frogs* (Oxford, 1908).

[8] M. P. Nilsson, *Greek Popular Religion* (Columbia Univ. Press, 1947) 3 ff., 20 ff.

[9] Plato, *Euthyphro* 14E 6–8: Ἐμπορικὴ ἄρα τις ἂν εἴη, ὦ Εὐθύφρων, τέχνη ἡ ὁσιότης θεοῖς καὶ ἀνθρώποις παρ' ἀλλήλων.—Ἐμπορική, εἰ οὕτως ἥδιόν σοι ὀνομάζειν.

[10] *Anth. Pal.* VII 694; the translation is by J. W. Mackail. With verse 3 εἰπεῖν οἷον ἐπ' ἔργον ἄγεις πόδας κτλ. compare the god συνεργός, Ar. *Eq.* 588 (Νίκη, in a prayer to Athena), Eur. *Med.* 396 (Hecate), *Hipp.* 523 (Cypris), *Ion* 48 (Apollo), and cf. Ehrenberg, *op. cit.* (in note 1 *supra*) 254, 1. Observe also the god σύμμαχος, Archilochus fr. 75 Diehl (Hephaistos), Eur. *Heraclid.* 766 ff. (Zeus), *Suppl.* 628 ff. (Zeus), and also the very frequent formulae σὺν θεῷ (or θεοῖς), οὐκ ἄνευ θεοῦ, οὐ θεῶν ἄτερ, and the like.

[11] Plato, *Phaedrus* 229A 8 ff. and 230B 2 ff.

[12] *Ibid.* 279B 8 ff.; the translation is H. N. Fowler's (*L.C.L.*).

[13] Nilsson, *op. cit.* (in note 8 *supra*) 65 ff.; also in *Griechische Religion*, I, 378 ff., and "Die Götter des Symposion," *Symbolae Danielsson* (Uppsala, 1932) 218 ff.

[14] Theophrastus, *Char.* 16.10.

[15] Theophr. ap. Porphyr. *de Abst.* 2.16 (Nauck) 145 ff. Cf. the daily offerings of frankincense by the physician Nicias to a cedar-wood statue of Asklepios, Theocr. Epigr. 8 (*Anth. Pal.* VI 33.7); cf. also M. P. Nilsson, "Pagan Divine Service in Late Antiquity," *Harv. Theol. Rev.* XXXVIII (1945) 64, and the story of Lycomedes, "praetor of the Ephesians," who sets up in his own bedchamber the portrait of John the Apostle and honors it with garlands, lamps, and altars (M. R. James, *The Apocryphal New Testament* [Oxford, 1945] 233). In the second century A.D., Apuleius says that Aemilianus has no piety because: nullum in villa eius delubrum situm, nullus locus aut lucus consecratus. "Et quid ego de luco et delubro loquor? Negant vidisse se qui fuere unum saltem in finibus eius aut lapidem unctum aut ramum coronatum." *Apologia* 56.5–6. (Sic Helm; *in finibus eius* post *fuere* transposuit Kroll.)

[16] Cf. Wilamowitz in his edition of the *Hippolytus* (Berlin, 1891), pp. 26 ff.

[17] This translation is by Gilbert Murray, as are also the other translations from the *Hippolytus* appearing in this chapter; see his Euripides in English (Oxford, 1902).

[18] Perhaps Euripides is hinting at this, *Hippol.* 79 f.: ὅσοις διδακτὸν μηδέν, ἀλλ' ἐν τῇ φύσει / τὸ σωφρονεῖν εἴληχεν.

[19] *Op. cit.* (in note 16 *supra*). Much more profound the view of Professor I. M. Linforth in his "Hippolytus and Humanism," *TAPhA* XLV (1914) 5 ff. and esp. 10 ff. I believe also myself that the punishment of Hippolytus is due to a "sin" against Aphrodite, the goddess being the exponent of the general law of love imposed on mankind. I am firmly convinced, further, that Hippolytus is not "in the slightest degree an ascetic" (Linforth, *loc. cit.* 12). But in my opinion the "sin" of Hippolytus is due more to his extreme youth than to a sort of abnormality ("inhuman continence," Linforth, *loc. cit.* 12), which I find really unthinkable in a Greek. In that case he would be a *monstrum*, and how could he interest the audience?

We should perhaps bear in mind certain facts. (1) The Greeks had no real sexual morality. To a boy in trouble Epicurus says that he may go on, provided he does not ruin his health or break some social custom. It would not have mattered to anybody if a grown-up boy, once free from the tutelage of a paedagogus, had had physical intercourse with a slave girl or a hetaera, or, for that matter, with another boy, or even a man, provided the man was of the same class and the boy was not venal. Hence I cannot see how the idea of "inhuman continence" could occur to a Greek mind. (2) On the other hand, boys of fifth-century Athens were not submitted, as are modern boys, to the constant excitement of mixing with girls, nor to the heavy sexual propaganda of magazines, advertisements, theater, cinema, radio, and the like. And it is a fact that college boys, living exclusively among boys, interested in hunting, games, and sports competitions, are not perpetually thinking of love for the other sex; indeed, they can even be shy of the other sex. (3) The strange mixture of friendship and love that we find in Plato's blushing boys has nothing to do with Aphrodite, who, for the Greek, presides over the relations between man and woman. On the other hand, it would be rash to label it immediately with the name of homosexuality. It could be often enough a sort of romantic love, an affair of the heart rather than of the senses. All considered, I would prefer to put Hippolytus in the category of these blushing boys than admit that, being inclined toward physical intercourse with the other sex, he still represses himself. This is something I believe a Greek could not have understood.

Now what is exactly Hippolytus' "sin" against Aphrodite? That this very purity for which, I repeat, he is not responsible because of his extreme youth, he believes to be a kind of privilege grounded in his own nature. (Cf. the quotation in the immediately preceding note.) Thence he has contempt for pleasures he has not yet enjoyed simply because he has not yet felt the need of them. This again, if I am not mistaken, is a proof that he is very young. An older boy would be so far sensible of the difficulty that he would try to bridle his sensuality, and therefore would be more humble.

Besides, we may note that among Euripidean boys Hippolytus is not the only one of the "anaphrodisischen Typus," to employ the term of W. Schmid, *Geschichte der griechischen Literatur*, I 3, 1 (Munich, 1940) 646, 2. We have also Ion, Parthenopaios (*Suppl.* 888 ff.), Achilles (*I.A.* 805, 830).

Moreover, the case of Hippolytus is not unique, and we have perhaps a typical legend. Cf. Ps.-Plut. *de Fluviis* 14.1: Τάναις . . . σωφρονέστατος ὑπάρχων τὸ γυναικεῖον γένος ἐμίσει, μόνον Ἄρη σεβόμενος· ἐν ἀτιμίᾳ δ' εἶχε καὶ τὸ γαμεῖν. ἡ δ' Ἀφροδίτη ἐπιθυμίαν αὐτῷ τῆς μητρὸς ἐνέσκηψεν. ὁ δὲ κατ' ἀρχὰς μὲν ἀντεμάχετο τῷ πάθει· νικώμενος δὲ ὑπὸ τῆς ἀνάγκης τῶν οἴστρων καὶ εὐσεβὴς διαμεῖναι βουλόμενος, ἑαυτὸν ἔρριψεν εἰς τὸν' Ἀμαζόνιον ποταμόν,—which, from then on, was named Tanais. See also Theocr. I 66 ff. (and D. S. IV 84 μυθολογοῦσι δὲ τὸν Δάφνιν μετὰ τῆς Ἀρτεμίδος κυνηγετεῖν ὑπηρετοῦντα τῇ θεῷ κεχαρισμένως) and Philostr. *V. Soph.* II 1, 12–16 (story of Agathion, the strange wild boy discovered by Herodes Atticus). This type of legend should be studied.

[20] For αἰδώς and σωφροσύνη cf. Eurip. *Hippol.* 78 ff.: Αἰδὼς δὲ ποταμίαισι κηπεύει δρόσοις / ὅσοις κτλ., as in note 24 *infra*. Cf. also Thucydides 1.84.3 where Archidamus addresses the Lacedaemonians: πολεμικοί τε καὶ εὔβουλοι διὰ τὸ εὔκοσμον γιγνόμεθα, τὸ μὲν ὅτι αἰδὼς σωφροσύνης πλεῖστον μετέχει, αἰσχύνης δὲ εὐψυχία. Add Plato, *Charm.* 160E 2 ff.: δοκεῖ τοίνυν μοι . . . αἰσχίνεσθαι ποιεῖν ἡ σωφροσύνη . . . καὶ εἶναι ὅπερ αἰδὼς ἡ σωφροσύνη.

[21] Cf. the ἀρχαία παιδεία in which σωφροσύνη 'νενόμιστο (Ar. *Nub.* 962); also, 992–993: κἀπιστήσει . . . / . . . τοῖς αἰσχροῖς αἰσχίνεσθαι, κἂν σκώπτῃ τίς σε φλέγεσθαι, and, 994–995: ἄλλο τε μηδὲν / αἰσχρὸν ποιεῖν, ὅ τι τῆς αἰδοῦς μέλλει τ' ἄγαλμ' ἀναπλήσειν. On the idea of αἰδώς in tragedy, cf. Wilamowitz, *Herakles*, 2d ed. (1895) II, 129 ff. ad v. 557; also Eurip. *Med.* 439.

[22] τὸ κοσμίως πάντα πράττειν καὶ ἡσυχῇ, Plato, *Charm.* 159B 3.

²³ Cf. note 20 *supra*.

²⁴ *Hippol.* 78: 'Αἰδὼς δὲ ποταμίαισι κήπευει δρόσοις. δρόσος is not only pure water or dew, but the down on fruit or on a young man; cf. Ar. *Nub.* 978–979 : ὥστε / τοῖς αἰδοίοισι δρόσος καὶ χνοῦς ὥσπερ μήλοισιν ἐπήνθει.

²⁵ *Hippol.* 998–999: ἀλλ' οἷσιν αἰδὼς μήτ' ἐπαγγέλλειν κακὰ / μήτ' ἀνθυπουργεῖν αἰσχρὰ τοῖσι χρωμένοις. Cf. also the quotations from *Nub.* in note 21 *supra*.

²⁶ *Hippol.* 17: Παρθένῳ ξυνὼν ἀεί. Wilamowitz in his edition of *Hippolytus* (cf. note 16 *supra*), p. 187, sees here a nasty innuendo. This seems to me nonsense. If Hippolytus were the lover of Artemis in a physical sense, he would be given up to Aphrodite, and in that case he is no more ἀνεπαφρόδιτος. What angers Aphrodite is that Hippolytus has, like Artemis herself, no inclination for physical love.

²⁷ Σκυθρωπὸς δὲ ἦν τὸ ἦθος καὶ ἀμειδὴς καὶ φεύγων τὰς συνουσίας. S.v. Εὐριπίδης, Suidas, p. 468.20 (Adler).

NOTES TO CHAPTER II
The Two Currents in Personal Religion
Reflective Piety: The Quest of God
(Pages 19–36)

¹ Soph. *Trach.* 1275–1278. The translation is that of C. M. Bowra, *Sophoclean Tragedy* (Oxford, 1944) 158. On this passage cf. H. Fränkel, *Dichtung und Philosophie des fruhen Griechenlands* (Philol. Monogr. Am. Philol. Assoc. No. XIII, 1950) 495, 35, 504 f., who compares Heraclitus fr. 67 Diels.

² The translation is derived from Ed. Fraenkel in his monumental edition (Oxford, 1950) of the *Agamemnon* (Vol. I).

³ *Od.* 6.41–46. The translation is Lawrence's, No. 44 (i) in *The Oxford Book of Greek Verse in Translation* (1938), ed. T. F. Higham and C. M. Bowra.

⁴ *Il.* 24.518 and 522–526. The translation is by Bridges, No. 36 in Higham and Bowra (*op. cit.* in preceding note).

⁵ Homeric *Hymn to Demeter* 147 ff., see No. 78 in Higham and Bowra (*op. cit.* in note 3 *supra*); the translation is by Call and Higham.

⁶ Cf. W. C. Greene, *Moira* (Harvard Univ. Press, 1944) 42 and n. 189, 170 ff.

⁷ Soph. *O.C.* 1224–1227. The translation is by W. B. Yeats in his *Collected Poems* (London, Macmillan, 1933), p. 262.

⁸ *Od.* 4.563, πείρατα γαίης.

⁹ Soph. fr. 870 (Nauck). The translation is Gilbert Murray's, No. 343 in Higham and Bowra (*op. cit.* in note 3 *supra*).

¹⁰ Hesiod, *Works and Days* 109 ff. Cf. Greene, *op. cit.* (in note 6 *supra*) 402 ff. (App. 7).

¹¹ *Od.* 4.563 ff.

¹² Pindar, *Olymp.* II 61 ff. and *Threnos* (fr. 129 Schroeder).

¹³ Pindar, *Pyth.* X 37 ff.

¹⁴ Cf. note 9 *supra*.

¹⁵ *Od.* 6.42 ff. Cf. note 3 *supra*.

¹⁶ (a) Gods, *Od.* 6.43 ff.: οὔτ' ἀνέμοισι ... οὔτε ποτ' ὄμβρῳ/δεύεται οὔτε χιὼν ἐπιπίλναται, ἀλλὰ μάλ' αἴθρη / πέπταται ἀνέφελος, λευκὴ δ' ἐπιδέδρομεν αἴγλη. (b) The Blessed, *Od.* 4.566 ff.: οὐ νιφετὸς οὔτ' ἄρ χειμὼν πολὺς οὔτε ποτ' ὄμβρος, / ἀλλ' αἰεὶ ζεφύροιο λιγὺ πνείοντος ἀήτας / Ὠκεανὸς ἀνίησιν ἀναψύχειν ἀνθρώπους. Also Pindar, *Ol.* II 61: ἴσαις δὲ νύκτεσσιν αἰεί, ἴσαις δ' ἀμέραις ἄλιον ἔχοντας ... and 70 ff. : ἔνθα μακάρων νᾶσον ὠκεανίδες αὖραι περιπνέοισιν, and *Threnos* (fr. 129 Schroeder): τοῖσι λάμπει μὲν σθένος ἀελίου τὰν ἔνθαδε νύκτα κάτω, φοινικορόδοις δ' ἐνὶ λειμώνεσσι προάστιον αὐτῶν καὶ λιβάνῳ σκιαρὸν καὶ χρυσέοις καρποῖς βεβριθός ... παρὰ δὲ σφισιν εὐανθὴς ἅπας τέθαλεν ὄλβος.

¹⁷ (a) Gods, *Od.* 6.46: τῷ ἔνι τέρπονται μάκαρες θεοὶ ἤματα πάντα. (b) The Blessed, *Od.* 4.565: τῇ περ ῥηΐστη βιοτὴ πέλει ἀνθρώποισιν. Also Hesiod, *Works and Days* 112 ff.: ὥστε θεοὶ δ' ἔζωον ἀκήδεα θυμὸν ἔχοντες / νόσφιν ἄτερ τε πόνων καὶ οἰζύος· οὐδέ τι δειλὸν / γῆρας ἐπῆν, αἰεὶ δὲ πόδας καὶ χεῖρας ὁμοῖοι / τέρποντ' ἐν θαλίῃσι κακῶν ἔκτοσθεν ἀπάντων, and Pindar, *Ol.* II 62 ff.: ἀπονέστερον ἐσλοὶ δέκονται βίοτον, οὐ χθόνα ταράσσοντες ἐν χερὸς ἀκμᾷ ... , ἀλλὰ παρὰ μὲν τιμίοις θεῶν οἵτινες ἔχαιρον εὐορκίαις ἄδακρυν νέμονται αἰῶνα. Also Pindar, *Pyth.* X 41 ff.: νόσοι δ' οὔτε γῆρας οὐλόμενον κέκραται ἱερᾷ γενεᾷ· πόνων δὲ καὶ μαχᾶν ἄτερ οἰκέοισι φυγόντες ὑπέρδικον Νέμεσιν.

¹⁸ θαλίαι. Cf. Hesiod *Works and Days*, 115: τέρποντ' ἐν θαλίῃσι, and *Od.* 11.602 f.: αὐτὸς (Heracles) δὲ μετ' ἀθανάτοισι θεοῖσι / τέρπεται ἐν θαλίῃς.

¹⁹ Cf. Hesiod, *Works and Days* 112: ὥστε θεοὶ ἔζωον ἀκήδεα θυμὸν ἔχοντες, and, for the gods, *Il.* 24.525 f.: ὡς γὰρ ἐπεκλώσαντο θεοὶ δειλοῖσι βροτοῖσι / ζώειν ἀχνυμένους· αὐτοὶ δέ τ' ἀκήδεές εἰσι.

²⁰ παρὰ τιμίοις θεῶν. See the context, Pindar, *Ol.* II 62 ff. as given in note 17 *supra*.

21 The translation is my own. For ἀπρόσδεικτος οἰόφρων I was assisted by Tucker's commentary (London, 1889).

22 Eurip. *Ion* 796 ff. The translation is that of A. S. Way (*L.C.L.*).

23 In his edition of the *Hippolytus*, p. 217.

24 The translation is by E. P. Coleridge in W. J. Oates and E. O'Neill, Jr., *The Complete Greek Drama* (New York, Random House, 1938) Vol. I, p. 783, except for the versions of Ἑσπερίδων . . . τᾶν ἀοιδῶν (742 f.), ὁ ποντομέδων (743), αὔξει . . . εὐδαιμονίαν θεοῖς (749 ff.), which are my own. I am also responsible for the capital "E" in Earth.

25 *Bacchae* 72 ff.: ὦ / μάκαρ, ὅστις εὐδαίμων / . . . / βιοτὰν ἁγιστεύει καὶ / θιασεύεται ψυχάν. The translation is by E. R. Dodds in his *Bacchae* (Oxford, 1944), p. 72. The division of lines (Ionic a minore) is that of Gilbert Murray in *O.C.T.*, but I would prefer, with Wilamowitz, to treat them as choriambic dimeter.

26 Exodus 21:24.

27 Aesch. *Agam.* 1527: ἄξια δράσας, ἄξια πάσχων.

28 Aesch. *Choeph.* 306 ff. This is my own translation, based substantially on the version by W. and C. E. S. Headlam in *The Plays of Aeschylus* (London, Bell, 1909).

29 II Samuel 12:1 ff. and esp. 11.

30 Hesiod, *Works and Days* 208 ff. The translation is that of Sir William Morris, No. 61 in Higham and Bowra (*op. cit.* in note 3 *supra*).

31 Hesiod, *Works and Days* 238 ff.

32 Aesch. *Suppl.* 1 ff. My own translation.

33 *Suppl.* 524 ff. My own translation.

34 Aesch. *Agam.* 58 ff.

35 Cf. Jeremiah 31:29 ff.: ἐν ταῖς ἡμέραις ἐκείναις οὐ μὴ εἴπωσιν Οἱ πατέρες ἔφαγον ὄμφακα, καὶ οἱ ὀδόντες τῶν τέκνων ἡμωδίασαν. ἀλλ' ἢ ἕκαστος ἐν τῇ ἑαυτοῦ ἁμαρτίᾳ ἀποθανεῖται, καὶ τοῦ φαγόντος τὰ ὄμφακα αἱμωδιάσουσιν οἱ ὀδόντες αὐτοῦ.

36 Theognis 731 ff. The translation is by J. M. Edmonds (*L.C.L.*). One would like to know the date of this piece. But the problem of "Theognis" is as confused today as of old. For J. Kroll, *Theognis-Interpretationen* (Leipzig, 1936), almost no part of the *Theognidea* comes from Theognis himself and so can be dated as of the sixth century. (On the rather wavering method of Kroll cf. H. Fränkel, *AJP* [1937] 235 ff.). T. W. Allen thinks that nearly all, if not all, comes from Theognis (*Proc. Brit. Acad.* XX [1934]). For style and

ideas 731 ff. is connected with 373 ff.; note the two invocations, Ζεῦ πάτερ 731 = Ζεῦ φίλε 373. Now Kroll thinks that the ideas of 373 ff. cannot be earlier than Euripides and the Sophists. For Fränkel, on the other hand (*op. cit. supra* 239, 2), the passage 384–392 is "a rondo composition, truly archaic and admirably finished but impossible in classical style," and 373–392, which makes a whole, except the interpolation 381–382, must be dated before 500 B.C., that is, previous to the Persian Wars and Aeschylus. In that case the parallel 731 ff. would also have to be reckoned previous to 500 B.C.

[37] Aesch. *Suppl.* 86 ff., 93 ff. My own translation, which includes, however, two suggestions from Professor Frederic Peachy (Berkeley). With ἵμερος . . . οὐκ εὐθήρατος (87) and πραπίδων πόροι κατιδεῖν ἄφραστοι (95) cf. *Troiades* 885, δυστόπαστος εἰδέναι.

[38] Aesch. *Agam.* 160 ff. The translation is by Ed. Fraenkel, *op. cit.* (in note 2 *supra*).

[39] Eurip. *Troiades* 884 ff. My own translation. On this passage, full of reminiscences of the fifth century's philosophy, cf. my *L'Enfant d'Agrigente*, 2d ed. (Paris, 1950) 17 f. and 172 f.

[40] Aesch. *Agam.* 176 ff. The translation is by Ed. Fraenkel, *op. cit.* (in note 2 *supra*).

[41] *Agam.* 206–208.

[42] *Il.* 19.86 ff. See the penetrating discussion by E. R. Dodds, *The Greeks and the Irrational* (Univ. of California Press, 1951).

[43] Aesch. *Choeph.* 910. On this evolution from the god αἴτιος to the god παραίτιος cf. Ed. Fraenkel's edition of the *Agamemnon*, II (Oxford, 1950), 373 ff.

[44] That is the real meaning of ἠεροφοῖτις Ἐρινύς in *Il.* 19.87.

[45] *Il.* 19.91.

[46] Aesch. *Agam.* 182 ff.: δαιμόνων δέ που χάρις βιαίως σέλμα σεμνὸν ἡμένων. I follow the interpretation of Ed. Fraenkel, *Agamemnon*, II, 108–112.

[47] Eurip. *Heracles* 1220 ff. For this, as for the following passages, the translator is Gilbert Murray.

[48] *Ibid.* 1227 ff.

[49] *Ibid.* 1351.

[50] *Ibid.* 1348.

[51] *Ibid.* 1357.

[52] *Stoic. Vet. Fragm.* I, No. 527. The translation is by C. C. Martindale, No. 484 in Higham and Bowra (*op. cit.* in note 3 *supra*).

[53] This fragment and those following are quoted according to Diels-Kranz.

[54] Cf. R. Pfeiffer, "Gottheit und Individuum," *Philologus* LXXXIV (1928–1929) 140 f.

[55] Fr. 94 Diehl (88 in Edmonds, *Elegy and Iambus*, II [*L.C.L.*]).

[56] Fr. 67A Diehl (66 Edmonds).

[57] Cf. H. Fränkel, *op. cit.* (in note 1 *supra*) 494, on fr. 67 Diels.

[58] θυμέ, θύμ' ἀμηχάνοισι κήδεσιν κυκώμενε, fr. 67A Diehl, 66 Edmonds. On the idea of ἀμηχανίη cf. Pfeiffer, *loc. cit.* (in note 54 *supra*). ἀνηκέστοισι κακοῖσιν, 7 Diehl and 9 Edmonds.

[59] Sallustius 21.36.15 ff., ed. A. D. Nock.

NOTES TO CHAPTER III

The Hellenistic Mood and
the Influence of Plato
(Pages 37–52)

[1] M. N. Tod, *Greek Historical Inscriptions* (Oxford, Vol. I, 2d ed., 1946; Vol. II, 1948) I, No. 30.

[2] On the date cf. W. S. Ferguson, *Hellenistic Athens* (London, Macmillan, 1911) 118.

[3] Cf. A. J. Festugière, *Contemplation et vie contemplative selon Platon*, 2d ed. (Paris, Vrin, 1950) 378, 406.

[4] Cf. Demetrius of Phalerum, frr. 79–81 Wehrli, translated by Gilbert Murray in *Five Stages of Greek Religion* (Thinker's Library, London, 1925), p. 133 n. 2.

[5] A. J. Festugière in *Harv. Theol. Rev.* XLII (1949) 209 ff., 223, 233 ff. Today I should no longer say that these last verses on Heimarmene are a late addition (233 ff.). After all, the *astrological* doctrine of Heimarmene must have been common since the beginning of Greco-Egyptian astrology (third cent. B.C.), and, as the authors of these Isiac aretalogies are very probably Greco-Egyptian priests of Isis, they could easily conceive Isis as a Savior in that matter as in all else.

⁶ Cf. the portrait of the true philosopher, *Theaet.* 172C ff., esp. 173E 4 ff. (ἡ δὲ διάνοια . . . πανταχῇ πέτεται κτλ.) and 175B 9 ff. (ὅταν δέ γέ τινα αὑτὸς . . . ἑλκύσῃ ἄνω κτλ.).

⁷ Plato, *Symp.* 211A–C. Cf. my work, cited in note 3 *supra*, 229 ff. on οὐδέ τις λόγος οὐδέ τις ἐπιστήμη, *Symp.* 211A 7.

⁸ Cf. Plato, *Laws* X 895D 4–E 8.

⁹ *Timaeus* 90A–D. Cf. F. M. Cornford, *Plato's Cosmology* (London, Routledge and Kegan Paul, 1937) 353 ff.

¹⁰ A. E. Taylor, "Plato and the Author of the Epinomis," *Proc. Brit. Acad.* XV (1929), and H. Raeder, *Platons Epinomis* (Det Kgl. Danske Vidensk. Selskab. Hist.-filol. Medd. XXVI, 1 [1928]).

¹¹ *Laws* X 903C 4–C 5. The translation is that of R. G. Bury (*L.C.L.*).

¹² Cf. already Anaximander, fr. 11 Diels, with the commentary of H. Fränkel in his *Dichtung und Philosophie* (see above, chap. ii, note 1), p. 347: "Wenn man aufs Ganze sieht, hat alles seine Richtigkeit."

¹³ A. J. Festugière, "L'Epinomis et l'introduction des cultes étrangers à Athènes," *Coniectanea Neotestamentica*, XI (1947) 66 ff.

¹⁴ The translation is that of C. M. Bowra, No. 322 in *The Oxford Book of Greek Verse in Translation*, ed. Higham and Bowra. Cf. *O.T.* 863 ff.

¹⁵ An *active* resignation, not a passive one. Cf. H. Fränkel, *op. cit.* (in note 12 *supra*), on τολμᾶν of Theognis (vv. 355 ff., 441 ff., 555 f., 591 ff.): "Was bleibt da noch übrig? Nichts anderes als was man sich selber geben kann: eine spezifische Form von Mut und Widerstand, die im Griechischen τολμᾶν genannt wird. . . . Gemeint ist Fassung und feste Haltung; ein Trotz, der den niedergedrückten Geist wieder aufrichtet; eine aktive Geduld, die den Geschwächten stärkt und dem Gefesselten die Freiheit wiedergibt."

NOTES TO CHAPTER IV
The Inclination to Retirement
(Pages 53–67)

¹ For a more general study of the subject cf. A. J. Festugière, *La Révélation d'Hermès Trismégiste* (Paris, Gebalda, 1944) I, 45 ff. Here I am limiting myself to the analysis of the word ἀναχώρησις.

² Note, however, Polybius 32.12.7, where with respect to a great lady

of Roman society, the mother of Scipio Africanus, ἀναχωρεῖν already means withdrawal from the world: διὸ τὸν πρὸ τοῦ χρόνον ἀνακεχωρη- κυίας αὐτῆς ἐκ τῶν ἐπισήμων ἐξόδων.

[3] A. J. Festugière, *Epicure et ses Dieux* (Paris, Les Presses Universi- taires, 1946). Note also *Kuriai Doxai* 14: τῆς ἀσφαλείας τῆς ἐξ ἀνθρώ- πων γενομένης . . . εἰλικρινεστέρα (Muehll, -εστάτη codd.) ἡ ἐκ τῆς ἡσυχίας καὶ ἐκχωρήσεως τῶν πολλῶν ἀσφάλεια.

[4] Ed. Jensen (Leipzig, Teubner, 1906), col. xxii, lines 18 ff. (pp. 61 ff.)

[5] κατὰ σοφίαν οὐδετέραν in *loc. cit.* in preceding note, col. xxii, line 25. The reference appears to me to be to (1) the wisdom of the contem- plative life and (2) the wisdom of the practical life; cf. lines 38 ff., ἐργάται τε τῶν καλῶν . . . καὶ θεωρηταί.

[6] A curious passage, full of classical echoes, for it records the criticism already addressed to contemplatives in the fifth century b.c. Cf. my *Contemplation . . . selon Platon*, pp. 35 ff.

[7] In col. xxiii, lines 4–18 (p. 64 Jensen). Philodemus approves too the πορισμός of income from rented flats or apartment houses (συνοικία, Lat. *insula*, but in Petron. 93.3 *synoecium*) or from the exploitation of slave labor in factories. "But all that holds only second or third rank. The most important and the most excellent is to receive gratitude with every sort of reverence, as Epicurus did, in exchange for philosophical discourses given to persons capable of understanding them, but for real, not polemical, discourses—in a word, for discourses not charged with excitement (ἀταράχων), since, moreover, to be a sophist and a logic-chopper is no better than to be a demagogue or a sycophant." Col. xxiii, lines 22–36 (p. 65 Jensen).

[8] I am sorry to have known too late the translation of Miss Cora E. Lutz, "Musonius Rufus 'The Roman Socrates,' " *Yale Classical Studies* X (1947) 33 ff. (the Greek text is that of Hense). For our fragment, cf. her pp. 81 ff.

[9] Stobaeus' extract begins with an ἔστι καὶ ἕτερος πόρος, but ἕτερος for ἄλλος is an abnormality frequent in the Koiné. Cf. Blass-Debrünner, p. 306, Moulton-Milligan s.v., and besides, later on in Stobaeus (p. 60.15 Hense), ἢ ἑτέρου δεῖσθαι τοῦ τρέφοντος.

[10] On this fact well known to historians of Hellenistic and Roman Egypt cf. Claire Préaux, *Economie royale des Lagides* (Brussels, 1939) 500 ff.; Rostovtzeff, *Social and Economic History of the Hellenistic World* (Oxford, 1941), Index, s.v. ἀναχώρησις, ἀνακεχωρηκότες, *Seces-*

sion. For the Roman period the same author, *Gesellschaft und Wirt-schaft*, Index, s.v. ἀναχώρησις. I may mention that Dittenberger, *Sylloge*, 3d ed., III, 310 ff., inscr. 1168 (2d ed., II, 649 ff., inscr. 802), line 118: τοῦτο ποιήσας εἰς τὸ ἄβατον ἀνεχώρησε (quoted by Moulton-Milligan, s.v. ἀναχωρέω, in this context), has nothing to do with the question; there it is the case of Asclepius' snake at Epidaurus which, after having healed a sick man, returns to its hole.

11 Sic U. Wilcken; cf. note 29 following.

12 On Socrates as a contemplative cf. *Contemplation . . . selon Platon*, pp. 69–73; on the narrative in the *Symposium* cf. *ibid.*, p. 69 n. 5.

13 ἑαυτῷ πως προσέχοντα τὸν νοῦν, *Symposium* 174D 5. This expression is almost the same as ἀναχωρεῖν εἰς ἑαυτόν. Cf. Seneca, *EM* 56.5: animum enim cogo sibi intentum esse.

14 No. XX in H. von Arnim's *Dionis Prusaensis quem vocant Chrysostomum quae exstant omnia* (Berlin, 1893) II, 259–268.

15 Arnim, *loc. cit. supra* 261.31–32. Yet, even so, they do not sleep, not for very long, anyway (*ibid.* 261.9–11). Cf. Seneca, *EM* 56.7. The mention of the sound of the waves to which one has become accustomed appears also in this *Discourse* of Dio's (262.4–8) and in Seneca, *EM* 56.3: ego istum fremitum [of and around his lodgings] non magis curo quam fluctum aut deiectum aquae.

16 Arnim, *loc. cit. supra* 261.32–262.4.

17 *Ibid.* 261.4–9: ἐάν τ' ἐν νήσῳ μικρᾷ καὶ μόνος. This *relegatio* of an offender against the Caesar into a small island where he might be a solitary prisoner is a commonplace of early Imperial history. Dio himself experienced banishment from Italy under Domitian, 82–96. He regained his full liberty in 96 when Nerva became princeps.

18 ἀγροικίας. On the enjoyment of these *villae rusticae* cf. Rostovtzeff, "Hellenistische-römische Architekturlandschaft," *Röm. Mittheil.* XXVI (1911), and *Gesellschaft und Wirtschaft*, Index, s.v. *Villen*; P. Grimal, *Les Jardins romains* (Paris, de Boccard, 1943), esp. pp. 377 ff. (Les Jardins et la sensibilité romaine); F. Poulsen, *Römische Kulturbilder* (Copenhagen, 1949) 145 ff. (Land und Stadt).

19 μέμνησο τῆς ὑποχωρήσεως τῆς εἰς τοῦτο τὸ ἀγρίδιον ἑαυτοῦ. (Lucian, *Hippias* 5, uses the word ὑποχώρησις for a retiring place in a bathing establishment: οἰκήματα βαλανείῳ . . . πρεπωδέστατα, χαρίεσσαι . . . ὑποχωρήσεις). According to Farquharson in his commentary to Marcus Aurelius, II, 595, the emperor is thinking perhaps of Epicurus' garden, or alludes to the *mihi me reddentis agelli* of Horace, *Ep.* 1.14.1.

This does not seem probable to me, nor would I care to think of the villa of the Antonines at Alsium in Etruria (cf. Fronto, *Ep.* pp. 223 ff. Naber, and *P.-W.*, s.v. Alsium) on the beach, since the point is precisely this, that Marcus Aurelius cannot go to this place, as the whole context shows. This retreat is, in my opinion, Marcus Aurelius himself, his own soul, into which he can always retire. Cf. VIII 48: ἀκρόπολίς ἐστιν ἡ ἐλευθέρα παθῶν διάνοια· οὐδὲν γὰρ ὀχυρώτερον ἔχει ἄνθρωπος ἐφ' ὃ καταφυγὼν ἀνάλωτος λοιπὸν ἂν εἴη, and X 23: ἐναργὲς ἔστω ἀεὶ τὸ ὅτι ἐκεῖνος ὁ ἀγρός ἐστιν, καὶ πῶς πάντα ἐστὶ ταὐτὰ ἐνθάδε τοῖς ἐν ἄκρῳ ὄρει ἢ ἐπὶ τοῦ αἰγιαλοῦ ἢ ὅπου θέλεις. ἄντικρυς γὰρ εὑρήσεις τὰ τοῦ Πλάτωνος· "σηκὸν ἐν ὄρει," φησί, "περιβαλλόμενος" καὶ "βδάλλειν βληχήματα." (*Theaet.* 174DE. The meaning is: "Everything is always the same, either here [perhaps in camp?] or in some retreat in the mountains or on the seashore; the important thing is to put oneself in a fold and to milk his ewes.") Cf. also VII 28: εἰς ἑαυτὸν συνειλοῦ· φύσιν ἔχει τὸ λογικὸν ἡγεμονικὸν ἑαυτῷ ἀρκεῖσθαι δικαιοπραγοῦντι καὶ παρ' αὐτὸ τοῦτο γαλήνην ἔχοντι and III 7: ὁ γὰρ τὸν ἑαυτοῦ νοῦν καὶ δαίμονα καὶ τὰ ὄργια τῆς τούτου ἀρετῆς προελόμενος τραγῳδίαν οὐ ποιεῖ, οὐ στενάξει, οὐκ ἐρημίας, οὐ πολυπληθείας, δεήσεται. The real wise man is content with his lot, does not complain, does not require that his happiness shall change ceaselessly from solitude to the crowd and vice versa. Farquharson, *op. cit.*, II, 577, compares Seneca, *de Tranq.* 17.3: odium turbae sanabit solitudo, taedium solitudinis turba.

20 Philo does not use either ἀναχωρεῖν or ἀναχώρησις in the spiritual sense. But this in itself is unimportant because he uses many words derived from μόνος (e.g., μοναγρία, μοναστήριον), and has many passages involving the words ἔρημος, ἐρημία, to say nothing of his romantic picture of the Essenes and of the Therapeutae.

21 There are in Epictetus many figures derived from the palaestra, very few figures drawn from country life. Moreover, ἀναχωρεῖν is always used by Epictetus to signify the act of retiring somewhere (to escape some evil), not the action of retiring to a quiet life; cf. II 1, 8 and 10; II 12, 6; IV 1, 96. "If Caesar," says he, "for some reason becomes my enemy, where would it be best that I should go for my retreat (ἀναχωρῆσαι ποῦ ποτε κρεῖσσον)? To the desert (εἰς ἐρημίαν)? But would not this fever go with me?"

22 ἀποταττόμεθα ταῖς αἰσθήσεσι: also *Legum Allegoria* III 41 (αἰσθήσει ἀποτάξασθαι), 142 (Moses ὅλῃ τῇ γαστρὶ ἀποτάττεται), 145 (Moses refuses to satisfy his appetites καὶ τοῖς ἄλλοις πάθεσιν ἀποτάττεται),

238 (ὅταν ... ἡ ψυχὴ ... ἀποτάξηται τοῖς κατὰ σῶμα). This verb ἀποτάττεσθαι is missing in Leisegang's *Index*. Cf. Flavius Josephus, *Antiquitates Iudaicae* XI 6, 8: καὶ Ἐσθὴρ δὲ ἱκέτευε τὸν θεόν ... , ῥίψασα κατὰ τῆς γῆς ἑαυτήν, καὶ πενθικὴν ἐσθῆτα περιθεμένη, καὶ τροφῇ καὶ ποτῷ καὶ τοῖς ἡδέσιν ἀποταξαμένη : also Luke 14 : 33 : οὕτως οὖν πᾶς ἐξ ὑμῶν ὃς οὐκ ἀποτάσσεται πᾶσιν τοῖς ἑαυτοῦ ὑπάρχουσιν, οὐ δύναται εἶναι μου μαθητής. (Τὰ ὑπάρχοντα is here to be taken as a substantive, as in 12 : 33, πωλήσατε τὰ ὑπάρχοντα ὑμῶν and 12 : 44, ἐπὶ πᾶσιν τοῖς ὑπάρχουσιν αὐτοῦ καταστήσει αὐτόν. Cf. Blass-Debrünner, p. 413.3). Iamblichus, *de Vita Pythagorica* 3, 13 (pp. 10–11 ff. Deubner): οἰνοποσίᾳ τε καὶ κρεωφαγίᾳ καὶ ἔτι πρότερον πολυφαγίᾳ ἀποταξάμενος. This ascetic sense of ἀποτάττεσθαι, ἀπόταξις, will have great importance in the Christian spiritual literature (cf. H. Koch, *Quellen zur Geschichte der Askese unter dem Mönchtum* [Tübingen, 1933], Index), so much so that Apotactites and Apotaxamenes will designate a particular sect (cf. *ibid.*, No. 48, p. 57; *Dictionnaire d'archéologie chrétienne*, I 2, pp. 2604 ff. [A. Lambert]). Add to these the inscriptions published by W. M. Calder, *Anatolian Studies* (Manchester, 1923), pp. 85 f., No. 8: ἔνθα κατάκειτε (lege -ται) Ἀνίκητος πρεσβύτερος τῶν Ἀποτακτικῶν. On the various meanings of ἀπόταξις cf. *Reallexicon für Antike und Christentum*, I 4, pp. 558 ff. (But Julian, *Orationes* VII 224B, ἀποτακτίτας [not ἀποτακτιστάς] τινὰς ὀνομάζουσιν οἱ ... Γαλιλαῖοι has to be added to the paragraph about the Christians; the reference is to certain gyrovague monks whom Julian compares to the Cynics).

[23] ἵνα τι τῶν θέας ἀξίων κατανοήσω. Cf. Musonius, p. 58.19 Hense: the shepherd's life οὐκ ἀπείργει τὴν ψυχὴν ἐκλογίζεσθαί τι τῶν κρειττόνων.

[24] Cf. Epictetus III 13: τί ἐρημία καὶ ποῖος ἔρημος. Life ἐν ἡσυχίᾳ in the desert never seems to Epictetus an ideal one ought to strive for. In IV 4 he derides those who yearn after the tranquil life (τὸ ἐν ἡσυχίᾳ διάγειν). People say: "Oh, when shall I be in Athens, to live there, at last, at ease?" The man who makes this complaint is undone, for, if he does not gain his wish, he is unhappy and lives in anguish (IV 4, 35–36). "At Rome there is always tumult, so many greetings to make." But it is always possible to preserve one's tranquillity of soul (τὸ εὑροεῖν; cf. the Stoic εὔροια βίου), IV 4, 37.

[25] πιστοῦ καὶ αἰδήμονος καὶ ὠφελίμου: the two first epithets are frequently united by Epictetus, e.g., I 4, 20; I 28, 20 and 23; II 2, 4; II 9, 11 etc.

[26] On the same cf. I 12, 20: σὺ δ' ἀταλαίπωρος εἶ καὶ δυσάρεστος κἂν ...

μόνος ἦς, ἐρημίαν καλεῖς τοῦτο κτλ. Also IV 4, 25 : μὴ γίνου δυσάρεστος μηδὲ κακοστόμαχος πρὸς τὰ γινόμενα, saying σχολὴν οὐ θέλω, ἐρημία ἐστίν. That is the feeling of the normal man. Solitude is only for the bestial man, whose odor is a trial to others; cf. IV 11, 16: ἢ ἄπελθ' εἰς ἐρημίαν πού ποτε ἦς ἄξιος εἶ, καὶ μόνος διάγε, κατόζων σαυτοῦ.

[27] In fact, it is a question of temperament. Cf. on this point W. Capelle, "Altgriechische Askese," *Neue Jahrb. f. d. klass. Alt.* XXV (1910) 703–704, who has stated well the difference between Epictetus and Marcus Aurelius thus (p. 703): "Während Epiktet mit seinem Denken und Handeln . . . ganz im Diesseits wurzelt, kommt dem Imperator . . . immer wieder die Flüchtigkeit des Menschenlebens, die Vergänglichkeit alles Irdischen ergreifend zum Bewusstsein." The same writer ascribes this taste for ἀναχώρησις to the revival of Pythagorean dualism from the first century B.C. onward (pp. 704 ff.). But, to tell the truth, all moral schools were syncretized in the Imperial Age, and it was not so much a case of different dogmatic teachings as of a spontaneous consciousness derived naturally from the culture of the times.

[28] Observe the case of Plotinus' friend, the senator Rogatianus who became so indifferent to material things (εἰς τοσοῦτον ἀποστροφῆς τοῦ βίου τούτου προκεχωρήκει) that he sold all his possessions, dismissed all his servants, resigned all his offices, and did not even live any longer in his own house, but sought hospitality from one or another of his friends (Porphyrius, *Vita Plotini* 7, 31 ff. Henry Schwyzer).

[29] *Archiv fur Papyrusforschung*, V (1909–1913) 222.

[30] Origen *in Jeremiam*, Homily XX 8, p. 189.33 Klostermann (or p. 30.22 Koch).

[31] Origen *in Luc*, Homily XI, p. 80.5 ff. Rauer (or p. 30.27 Koch).

[32] ἐνθυμούμενος τὰς ἐν οὐρανῷ μονὰς τόν τε πόθον ἔχων εἰς αὐτὰς καὶ σκοπῶν τὸν ἐφήμερον τῶν ἀνθρώπων βίον.

NOTES TO CHAPTER V
Popular Piety
Lucius and Isis
(Pages 68–84)

Works of constant reference in this chapter are the following:

Bernhard, Max. *Der Stil des Apuleius von Madaura*, Tübinger Beiträge, 2 (Stuttgart, 1927).

Berreth, J. *Studien zum Isisbuch in Apuleius' Metamorphosen*, Diss. Tübingen (Tübingen, 1931).

Nock, A. D. *Conversion* (Oxford, 1933) 138 ff.

Reitzenstein, R. *Die Hellenistischen Mysterienreligionen*, 3d ed. (Berlin, 1927).

Wittmann, Willi. *Das Isisbuch des Apuleius*, Diss. Berlin (Stuttgart, 1938).

[1] Cf. I 2, 1: Thessaliam—nam et illic originis maternae nostrae fundamenta a Plutarcho illo inclito ac mox Sexto philosopho, nepote eius, prodita gloriam nobis faciunt. Lucian does not speak of this relationship. The indication comes probably from the Greek original.—"Traveling for business": ex negotio, I 2, 1.

[2] Extremae sortis quadrupedem, VII 3, 1; pessimae mihique iamdudum detestabilis beluae, XI 6, 2. The ass is especially loathsome to Isis since it is the beast of Typhon; cf. Plut. *Is. Os.* 30 ff., and Wittmann, n. 166. For the ἀσέλγεια of the ass cf. Olck ap. *P.-W.* VI, 634.64 ff. (Esel), and Semon. 7, 48 f. D: ὅμως δὲ καὶ πρὸς ἔργον ἀφροδίσιον / ἐλθόντ' ἑταῖρον ὁντινῶν ἐδέξατο. Also Pindar, *Pyth.* X 36: γελᾷ θ' (sc. Ἀπόλλων) ὁρῶν ὕβριν ὀρθίαν κνωδάλων (sc. ὄνων, 33).

[3] summatem deam praecipua maiestate pollere, XI 1, 2.

[4] On the composition of this prayer, Regina Caeli . . . ista luce feminea . . . redde me meo Lucio (XI 2, 1–4), cf. Bernhard 73, Berreth 11–19, Wittmann 9–15. Three triads (I, ista luce . . . lumina; II, tu meis . . . tribue; III, depelle . . . Lucio, separated by little "Zwischenstücke," (1) quoquo nomine . . . invocare; (2) sit . . . periculorum. The analysis of Wittmann is too complicated and he overdoes the "Zahlensymbolik." For *sive seu seu* and *quoquo nomine*, cf. Norden, *Agnostos Theos* (Leipzig, 1913) 144 ff., who quotes (144, 1) Ps.-Apul.

Asclepius 20 (320.11 N.-F.): deus . . . vel pater vel dominus omnium
vel quocumque alio nomine . . . nuncupatur.

[5] On the description of Isis, cf. Berreth 38–49, Wittmann 15–22.

[6] En adsum . . . totus veneratur orbis (XI 5, 1); cf. Bernhard 73,
Berreth 38–49, Wittmann 15–22. Three triads (I, rerum naturae . . .
progenies initialis; II, summa . . . caelitum; III, caeli . . . silentia.
Note the rhymes in II and III). The second and third triads
are separated by a Zwischenstück (deorum . . . quae). On Inde
primigenii . . . reginam Isidem (XI 5, 2–3) cf. Bernhard 86, and
Berreth and Wittmann *loc. cit. supra*. Two triads (I, Inde . . .
Venerem; II, Cretes . . . Cererem); two dyads, (1) Iunonem . . . alii,
(2) Hecatam . . . illi, solemn ending, et qui . . . Isidem. The plan
of the whole discourse 5.1–6.7 is as follows:

    I. En adsum tuis commota precibus (5.1), resumed by adsum
tuos miserata casus, adsum favens et propitia (5.4).

    II. Isis reveals herself as

        1. Ruler of the world, rerum naturae parens . . . dispenso
(5.1);

        2. Many-named goddess, cuius numen unicum . . . reginam
Isidem (5.1–3).

    III. Cheers Lucius: Adsum . . . dies salutaris (5.4).

    IV. Gives orders: ergo igitur *imperiis* istis meis (5.4):

        1. For Lucius' deliverance, diem qui dies . . . criminabitur
(5, 5–6, 6);

        2. For Lucius' new life, plane memineris . . . quod vives
(6, 5).

    V. Gives promises about this life and the next: vives autem
beatus . . . mihi tantum licere (6, 6–7).

    Compare the Isiac aretalogies (cf. *Harv. Theol. Rev.* XLII [1949]
209 ff.) and *Pap. Oxyrh.* 1380.

[7] tenacibus castimoniis (6.7); cf. note 32 *infra*.

[8] On the procession and the navigium Isidis cf. Berreth 50–100,
Wittmann 39–69, 90 ff.

[9] Wittmann's idea (72), "Symbolhaft legt ihm einer aus der Kohorte
der Geweihten den Mantel, d.h. den Leib der Gottheit um," is
nonsense. Lucius is given a garment because he is naked and is
ashamed of being so.

[10] "As . . . ecstasy": vultu geniali et hercules inhumano, XI 14, 5;
ad istum modum vaticinatus sacerdos . . . fatigatus anhelitus tra-

hens, XI 16, 1; a well-known commonplace, as e.g., Verg. *Aen.* 6.79
f. tanto magis ille (sc. Phoebus) *fatigat* / os rabidum.

[11] On the priest's discourse cf. Berreth, 101–106, and Wittmann,
77–90. On ad portum Quietis (15, 1) cf. for verbal parallel Ael.
Aristid. XLII (εἰς Ἀσκληπιόν) 1 (334.2 Keil): Ἀσκληπιὲ δέσποτα, ὡς
ἀσμένοις . . . ἔδωκας ἡμῖν οἷον ἐκ πελάγους πολλοῦ καὶ κατηφείας λιμένος τε
λαβέσθαι γαληνοῦ καὶ προσειπεῖν τὴν κοινὴν τῶν ἀνθρώπων ἑστίαν, and,
generally, Campbell Bonner, "Desired Haven," *Harv. Theol. Rev.*
XXXIV (1941) 49–67. On ad aram Misericordiae (*ibid.*) cf. Dittenberger, *Sylloge*, 3d ed., inscr. 1149 (Ἐλέου βωμός, Epidauros, Imperial
times); Ael. Aristid. εἰς Σάραπιν, XLVIII 26 K.; *I.G.* XIV 2413, 3: εἰς
Ζεὺς Σέραπις ἐλέησον. Cf. E. Peterson, Εἷς Θεός, 230.

[12] XI 17, 5 intentus ⟨in praesentis⟩ deae specimen; 19, 1 me rursum ad
deae . . . refero conspectum; 20, 4 dum . . . deae venerabilem conspectum adprecamur; 24, 5 inexplicabili voluptate simulacri divini
perfruebar.

[13] ipsamque traditionem ad instar voluntariae mortis et precariae
salutis celebrari, XI 21, 7.

[14] cultor adsiduus, 26, 3. Compare cultor inseparabilis, 19, 1.

[15] On the second initiation (to Osiris) and the third initiation (to
Isis), cf. Wittmann 121–130.

[16] Compare the promise of Asclepius to Aelius Aristides, L 13–30.

[17] The latest are, so far as I know, Berreth and Wittmann. H. Erbse,
"Griechisches und Apuleianisches bei Apuleius," *Eranos* XLVIII
(1950) 107 ff., has no special bearing on *Met.* XI.

[18] G. Lafaye, *Histoire du culte des divinités d'Alexandrie* (Paris, 1884)
110; F. Cumont, *Religions orientales*, 4th ed., p. 245 n. 106. P.
Foucart, *Mystères d'Eleusis* (Paris, 1914) 401 ff., is unwilling to
relate the Isiac mysteries too closely with the mysteries of Eleusis.

[19] K. H. E. de Jong, *De Apuleio isiacorum mysteriorum teste* (Leiden,
1900). Expanded in *Das antike Mysterienwesen* (Leiden, 1909),
where see esp. 203 ff.

[20] Reitzenstein 220–234. Same interpretation by Wittmann, who emphasizes the Egyptian elements of the rite, 112 ff., 117 ff. Berreth,
109 ff., compares *Met.* XI 23, 7 and the Mithrasliturgie (*Pap. Gr.
Magicae*, IV, 475–750). See lastly, in Vol. II (1950) of E. P. Nilsson's
Griech. Rel., pp. 606 ff.; he emphasizes the syncretistic elements in
the initiation.

[21] At least as to the details of the rite. The general meaning is given in

XI 15, 7 (the priest's discourse): ipsamque traditionem ad instar
voluntariae mortis et *precariae salutis* celebrari. It is a *death* and a
new birth. And this is precisely what we find in XI 23, 7 ff.: (a)
Death: accessi *confinium mortis* et calcato Proserpinae limine; (b)
New birth as Helios (24, 4–5): sic *ad instar solis* exornato me . . .
exhinc festissimum celebravi *natalem sacrorum*.

[22] So R. Helm, "Das Märchen von Amor und Psyche," *Neue Jahrb.*
XXXIII (1914) 175 ff.: "Dass . . . in Wahrheit das elfte Buch mit
der Mysteriendarstellung ein ganz unpassender dunkler Flicken ist
auf einem heiteren, hellen Gewande, ist meine feste Ueberzeugung.
Apuleius hat . . . einfach das griechische Original von den . . . Er-
lebnissen des Esel gewordenen Menschen . . . in seiner Sprache . . .
übertragen, ohne sich um den Ausgang der Geschichte zu kümmern,
und dann nur den Schluss abgeändert, um an alle die . . . pikanten
Ereignisse eine . . . eigene Lebenserfahrung zu knüpfen. Diese passt
nicht im mindesten zu der Einleitung." But *contra* the last con-
tributor is Erbse, 122 f. (See note 17 *supra*.) It is well known that
Lucian's *Ass* contains no parallel to *Met.* XI. In the *Ass* Lucius
becomes again a man at Thessalonica (49) just as he is about to be
presented in display at the theater (54 ff.).

[23] But already I 6, 4: Aristomene . . . , ne tu fortunarum lubricas
ambages et instabiles incursiones et reciprocas vicissitudines ig-
noras; I 7, 1: Sine, sine . . . , fruatur diutius *tropaeo Fortuna* quod
fixit ipsa. Conversely, XI 15, 4: Isidis magnae providentia gaudens
Lucius *de sua Fortuna triumphat*. Wittmann (n. 2) observes that
τύχη appears only once in Lucian's *Ass*, c. 47, and there as a pleasant
goddess: κἀγὼ τὴν Τύχην ὁρῶν ἤδη ἀπαλόν μοι προσμειδιῶσαν κτλ.
Compare *Met.* VII 20, 1: Sed in rebus scaevis adfulsit Fortunae
nutus *hilarior*, but with the addition nescio an futuris periculis me
reservans. Needless to say, this theme of Fortune (Τύχη) is quite
common in the Greek novel. Cf. E. Rohde, *Der griechische Roman
und seine Vorläufer* (1st ed., Leipzig, 1876), p. 493, 2; K. Kerényi,
Die griechisch-orientalische Romanliteratur (Tübingen, 1927), index,
s.v. Τύχη, and, for Apuleius, pp. 179 ff.

[24] Subibatque me non de nihilo veteris priscaeque doctrinae viros
finxisse ac pronuntiasse *caecam et prorsus exoculatam esse Fortunam*
(VII 2, 4), rursus in me *caecos* detorsit oculos (VIII 24, 1).

[25] *Divinae providentiae* fatalis dispositio (IX 1, 5). Divina providentia
is here Fortune's design, not Providence, as with the Stoics.

[26] XI 5, 4: Iam tibi *providentia mea inlucescit* dies salutaris; XI 12, 1: quod . . . deae maximae *providentia* adluctantem mihi saevissime Fortunam superarem; XI 15, 3: in tutelam iam receptus es Fortunae, *sed videntis* quae *suae lucis splendore* ceteros etiam deos *illuminat.*

[27] Apuleius comes again to this topic in Lucius' prayer, XI 25, 2: nec dies . . . quin . . . salutarem porrigas dexteram, qua *fatorum* etiam inextricabiliter contorta retractas licia et *Fortunae* tempestates mitigas.

[28] *Aretalogia Cymaea,* 55 f. Cf. W. Peek, *Der Isishymnus von Andros* (Berlin, 1930) 124: Ἐγὼ τὸ εἱμαρμένον νικῶ. Ἐμοῦ τὸ εἱμαρμένον ἀκούει. Compare numen invictum, XI 7, 1.

[29] The importance of the *curiositas* topic is well explained by Wittmann, 81 f., who quotes Ps.-Apul. *Asclep.* 14 (312.21 N.-F.): haec (the pietas) est *nulla animi importuna curiositate* violata philosophia.

[30] Cf., for instance, on the girls in the inns, F. Poulsen, *Römische Kulturbilder* (Copenhagen, 1949) 184 f.

[31] Cf. VIII 29, 5; Lucius loathes the extrema flagitia of the priests of the Dea Syria (nec diu tale facinus meis oculis tolerantibus etc.). In IX 27, 1–2 Lucius brings to punishment an adulterer, and in X 34, 5 he is ashamed to pollute his body with a wicked harlot. Again in XI 14, 4 Lucius is shy about appearing naked in public. In quite a contrary spirit Lucian, *Ass* 56: καὶ ἐξωσθεὶς πρὸ τοῦ δωματίου ἔξω γυμνὸς καλῶς . . . τὴν γῆν γυμνὴν περιλαβὼν ταύτῃ συνεκάθευδον. ἅμα δὲ τῷ ὄρθρῳ γυμνὸς ὢν ἔθεον ἐπὶ ναῦν καὶ λέγω πρὸς τὸν ἀδελφὸν τὸν ἐμαυτοῦ ἐν γέλωτι συμφοράν. The tone is quite different.

[32] XI 6, 7 (tenacibus castimoniis); XI 19, 3 (castimoniorum abstinentiam satis arduam). Like ἁγνεία the word *castimonia* (or *castimonium*) is ambiguous. It may mean abstinence from certain foods, and we know that the devotees of Isis were accustomed to undergo such abstinences (XI 21, 8), especially before the initiation (XI 23, 2; 28, 5; 30, 1). The phrase in XI 30, 1 is inanimae . . . castimoniae iugum subeo. But *castimonia* in the plural, without any associated determinative, seems at least to include also abstinence from sexual intercourse, and this is, after all, the primary sense of *castimonia* (cf. Livy, XXXIX 9, 4). If so, first, we understand better the *religiosa formido* of Lucius before the initiation (XI 19, 3). He has no fear of the ceremony in itself; it is only later that the priest explains to him how dreadful it is (XI 21, 6). Then he fears his inability to

sustain the ordinances of the new life and dreads breaking his *sacramentum* (XI 15, 5). Secondly, the more one reads the picture of Lucius' secluded life in the temple of Isis, the less one feels that such a life could tolerate voluptuous pastimes. Thirdly, this picture in *Met.* XI seems to constitute a literary contrast with the wanton life of Lucius in *Met.* II. On the chastity of the priests of Isis see as well K. H. E. de Jong, *Das antike Mysterienwesen*, 69 ff.

33 That Apuleius in the *Met.* speaks of himself was already the feeling of Augustine, *Civ. Dei* XVIII 18 (II 218, 5 ff. Dombart): Nam et nos cum essemus in Italia audiebamus talia de quadam regione illarum partium ubi inbutas his malis artibus in caseo dare solere dicebant quibus vellent seu possent viatoribus, unde in iumenta ilico verterentur et necessaria quaeque portarent postque perfuncta opera iterum ad se redirent; nec tamen in eis mentem fieri bestialem sed rationalem humanamque servari, sicut *Apuleius in libris quos asini aurei titulo inscripsit sibi ipsi accidisse, ut accepto veneno humano animo permanente asinus fieret, aut indicavit aut finxit.*

34 De eius ore . . . audisse mitti sibi *Madaurensem*, sed admodum pauperem. On this last point cf. Apuleius, *Apologia* 23, 1–2: profiteor mihi . . . relictum a patre HS viciens paulo secus, idque a me *longa peregrinatione et diutinis studiis et crebris liberalitatibus modice imminutum.* Compare *Met.* XI 28, 1: sumptuum tenuitate . . . retardabar. Nam et viriculas patrimonii peregrinationis adtriverant impensae.

35 Apul. *Apol.* 61 ff., esp. 61, 3.

36 Apul. *Apol.* 55, 8: sacrorum pleraque initia in Graecia participavi. Cf. *Met.* III 15, 4: qui . . . sacris pluribus initiatus profecto nosti sanctam silentii fidem.

37 About thirty years of age. Cf. P. Valette in his edition of the *Apologia* (Paris, 1924), p. vii.

38 Plane memineris . . . *mihi* reliqua vitae tuae curricula . . . *vadata.*

39 Crebris imperiis in XI 19, 2. Cf. XI 5, 4: imperiis istis meis; 22, 2: non obscuris imperiis; 22, 6: divinis imperiis; 29, 1: mirificis imperiis deum. For monitu see XI 19, 2. Cf. (all in XI) 6, 1: meo monitu; 24, 6: deae monitu; 26, 4: commonet; 27, 8: commonefactum.

40 neque *vocatus* morari nec *non iussus* festinare (XI 21, 5). For *iussus* cf. postremo iussus XI 28, 3.

41 noctis obscurae non obscuris *imperiis* evidenter *monuit* advenisse diem mihi semper optabilem (XI 22, 2).

[42] divinis imperiis, in XI 22, 6.

[43] XI 24, 6: deae monitu; 26, 1: deae potentis instinctu; 26, 4: commonet; 27, 6: post tam manifestam deum voluntatem; 28, 2: numinis premebar instantia; 29, 1: mirificis imperiis deum; 29, 3: sic
instruxit . . . clemens imago; 30, 1: pronuntiavit. Note that the
admonitions before the second initiation are admonitions of Isis
(XI 26, 4, numinis benefici cura pervigilis, whence *numinis* in 28,
2 designates Isis and *inquit* in 28, 4 has Isis for subject) or visions
sent by Isis (vision of the pastophorus in 27, 4 ff.). Before the third
initiation Lucius has one vision of Isis (*clemens imago* in 29, 3 and
suada maiestas in 30, 1) and one vision of Osiris himself (30, 3).
However, the orders for the second and the third initiation are said
to be orders of the two gods: post tam manifestam *deum* voluntatem (27, 6), imperiis *deum* (29, 1), *caelestium* . . . intentio (29, 2),
assidua ista *numinum* dignatione (29, 4), *deis* magnis auctoribus
(29, 5), because Lucius is to be henceforth a servant of Osiris (27, 3)
as well as of Isis.

[44] XI 21, 8: dignatione; 22, 5: dignatur; 29, 4: dignatione. The *oracu-
lum* of Isis (XI 5-6, 7, 1) is already a *dignatio* (4). On *dignatio*
and *vocatio* cf. Reitzenstein, 252 ff., and my *Idéal religieux des Grecs*
(Paris, 1932) 305, 6 (ἄξιος in the magical papyri).

[45] ut renatus quodam modo, statim sacrorum obsequio desponderetur.
As to Reitzenstein, 39, 262 ff., it should be noted that Lucius is here
reborn in so far as he becomes a *man* again after having been an *ass*;
cf. XI 16, 3: hunc . . . deae numen . . . *reformavit ad hominem*. Likewise in XI 21, 7: quippe cum transactis vitae temporibus iam in
ipso finitae lucis limine constitutos . . . numen deae soleat . . . *quodam modo renatos* ad novae reponere rursus salutis curricula, it is
not a question of "mystic birth," but of the fact that Isis can pro-
long human life beyond its usual course; cf. XI 6, 7: scies ultra
statuta fato tuo spatia *vitam quoque tibi prorogare mihi tantum
licere.* Man is *renatus* for a new term of temporal life, not for a divine
life given by a supernatural grace. Note in the two sentences
quodam modo; Lucius is "as it were" *renatus* when returning to the
human form; men are "as it were" *renati* when receiving a new term
of life. I see now that W. L. Knox, *Some Hellenistic Elements in
Primitive Christianity* (London, 1944) 91, offers the same interpretation.

[46] Moreover, this "macarismos" of the *omnes populi* (XI 16, 2) is a

liturgical formula. Cf. Berreth 102, Wittmann 87 ff., but the latter goes beyond the point.

[47] χεῖρας καθαρὸς καὶ φωνὴν συνετός, Celsus ap. Origen. *contra Celsum* III 59.

[48] Pausanias X 32, 13: "About forty furlongs from the temple of Aesculapius is [at Tithorea, in Phocis] an enclosure and sacred shrine of Isis, the holiest of all the sanctuaries made by the Greeks for the Egyptian goddess. For . . . there is no admission to the shrine save for those whom Isis herself has favored with an invitation in a dream." (οὓς ἂν αὐτὴ προτιμήσασα [cf. *dignatio, dignari*] ἡ Ἶσις καλέσῃ σφᾶς δι' ἐνυπνίων.) The translation is that of J. G. Frazer.

[49] Pausanias X 32, 17: "They say that once upon a time . . . a profane fellow who had no right to go down into the shrine, rashly entered it out of curiosity. The whole place seemed to him full of spectres; and scarcely had he returned to Tithorea . . . when he gave up the ghost." In X 32, 18 the same story is told about a profane man who entered the shrine of Isis at Coptus: "Thus it appears to be a true saying of Homer's that it is ill for mankind to see the gods in bodily shape." Both these translations are from Frazer.

[50] Acts of the Apostles 16: 9. Cf. A. Wikenhauser, *Die Traumgesichte des neuen Testaments in religionsgeschichtlicher Sicht* ap. *Pisciculi Fr. J. Dolger dargeboten* (Münster, 1939) 320 ff.

[51] Ael. Arist. XLVIII 72 ff.

[52] *Mihi* reliqua vitae tuae curricula . . . *vadata* in XI 6, 5. On the juridical word *vadata*, cf. Wittmann 84. Also 15, 2: eos quorum *sibi* vitas ⟨in⟩ *servitium* deae nostrae maiestas *vindicavit*. Also 27, 3: prohinc *me* quoque peti magno etiam deo *famulum sentire deberem*. In XI 15, 5 the *servitium* (deae servire) is compared to a military service (da nomen *sanctae* huic *militiae*). Compare also tunc e *cohorte* religionis unus 14, 5, and stipatum me religiosa *cohorte* 23, 1. On this cf. Reitzenstein 192 ff., and my *Idéal religieux des Grecs* (cited in note 44 *supra*) 305 (*militia* in the magical papyri).

[53] Cf. K. Holl, "Die Geschichte des Worts Beruf," *Sitz. Akad. d. Wiss. Berlin* XXIV (1924) xxix–lvii, or in *Kl. Schr.* III, 189 ff.

[54] XI 20, 3: templi matutinas apertiones opperiebar. Cf. also 22, 7: rituque sollemni apertionis celebrato ministerio; 27, 6: deae matutinis perfectis salutationibus. In XI 20, 4 we should perhaps keep *deae* and write *deae penetrali* fontem petitum spondeo libat. Cf. Wittmann 97–99, who observes (n. 529) that Apuleius never says

penetrale for the Holy of Holies, but always *penetralia*. Cf. III 5, 15 (metaphorical); XI 6, 6: Stygiisque *penetralibus* regnantem; 17, 1: qui venerandis *penetralibus* pridem fuerant initiati; 23, 4: ad ipsius sacrarii *penetralia*.

[55] XI 22, 1: intentus miti quiete et probabili taciturnitate.

[56] Professor A. D. Nock has kindly drawn my attention to the possibility that it could be an "act of devotion," comparing the "Jongleur de Notre Dame" and the conventional prayers (*tours de force*) inscribed on the temple of Talmis; cf. *Harv. Theol. Rev.* XXVII 1934) 60 ff. See also K. von Fritz, "Greek Prayers," *Review of Religion*, X (1945) 26: "Works of art . . . can be offerings to the gods regardless of the spiritual character of their content, merely because they are beautiful and expressions of man's highest creative ability." This prayer is on the "Du-Stil" of Norden, *Agnostos Theos* 149 ff. See also Bernhard 278 f. and Wittmann 130–139. We have here the series *tu . . . , te . . . , tu . . . , tibi . . . , tuo . . . , tuam* (XI 25, 1–4), afterward the conclusion *at ego . . . , ergo* (25, 5–6). As usual, Wittmann overemphasizes the Zahlensymbolik.

[57] Euripides, *Ion* 184 ff.

[58] Dio Chrys. XII. Cf. Ch. Clerc, *Les Théories relatives au Culte des Images chez les Auteurs Grecs du II⁰ siècle après Jésus-Christ* (Paris, n.d.) 171 ff. (On Dio, 194 ff.)

[59] Cf., for instance, A. D. Nock, "A Vision of Mandulis Aion," *Harv. Theol. Rev.* XXVII (1934) 53 ff.

NOTES TO CHAPTER VI

Popular Piety
Aelius Aristides and Asclepius
(Pages 85–104)

In general, cf. A. Boulanger, *Aelius Aristides et la Sophistique dans la province d'Asie au II⁰ siècle de notre ère* (Paris, 1923). On the life of Aristides see also Wilamowitz-Moellendorff, "Der Rhetor Aristeides," *Sitz. Berlin. Akad.*, phil.-hist. Klasse, XXX (1925) 333 ff. I was able to get only glimpses of Dr. C. A. de Leeuw's book, *Aelius Aristides als bron voor de kennis van zijn tijd* (Amsterdam, 1939).

On Aristides' religious experience cf. F. G. Welcker, "Incubation.

Aristides der Rhetor," *Kl. Schr.* III, 89 ff., esp. 114 ff., a fine study. See also the short paper of O. Weinreich, "Typisches und Individuelles in der Religiosität des Aelius Aristides," *Neue Jahrb.* XXXIII (1914) 597 ff. For the significance of the dreams in Aristides' cures, consult the excellent discussion of E. J. and L. Edelstein, *Asclepius* (Baltimore, 1945) II, 162–173. For some texts of Aristides and other texts concerning Asclepius, I used in part the same work, Vol. I (quoted by the numbers in this book). The first group of numbers used in quoting the *Discourses* of Aristides are those of Keil, the second those of Dindorf, Vol. I.

[1] We have from Aristides the following:

I. Eulogies of Athens (I), Rome (XXVI), Cyzicus (XXVII)
II. Ceremonial speeches on well-known topics:
    1) Concordia within the city (Rhodes, XXIV) or among cities (Pergamum, Smyrna, Ephesus, XXIII)
    2) Rhetoric and philosophy (II, LV)
    3) Moral problems: against comedy (to the Smyrneans, XXIX); against the dance (to the Spartiates: lost, cf. Schmid-Stählin, 700, 3)
III. *Meletai* or *declamations* about a mythical story or a historical fact:
    1) Agamemnon's deputation to Achilles, *Il.* IX (XVI)
    2) Peloponnesian War (VII–XIII)
    3) The politics of Athens after Leuctra (XI–XV)
    4) Athens and Philip II of Macedon (IX–X)
IV. Speeches in self-defense (XXVIII, XXXIII, XXXIV)
V. Funeral eulogies
    1) Of his teacher Alexander (XXXII)
    2) Of a pupil (XXXI)
VI. Eulogies of gods or sanctuaries (XXXVII–XLVI, LIII)
VII. Speeches about the earthquake of Smyrna in 178 (XVIII–XXI)
VIII. Sacred discourses (XLVII–LII)

[2] When Wilamowitz says (*loc cit. supra,* 341): "Ein Künstler hat darauf Anspruch nach seiner Kunst beurteilt zu werden, mindestens soweit, dass man seine persönliche Leistung würdigt, mag man auch die ganze Kunstrichtung ablehnen," or (342): "dem alten Künstler

sollen wir geschichtliche Gerechtigkeit angedeihen lassen und nicht Masstàbe an ihn legen, die er weder gekennt hat noch anerkennen würde," he is surely right as a historian of Greek prose. For all that, Aristides in his *meletai* is "unerträglich."

³ XLVII–LII Keil (XXIII–XXVIII Dindorf), the last one unfinished, two pages only.

⁴ Pausanias VIII 15, 4: κύαμον μὲν οὖν ἐφ' ὅτῳ μὴ καθαρὸν εἶναι νομίζουσιν ὄσπριον, ἔστιν ἱερὸς ἐπ' αὐτῷ λόγος. In the same chapter (15, 1–2), Pausanias says that there are at Pheneus "two great stones fitted to each other," and that "every year, when they are celebrating the Greater Mysteries, they open these stones and, taking out of them certain writings (γράμματα) which bear on the mysteries, they read them within the hearing of the initiated and put them back in their place the same night." (The translation is Frazer's, modified.) It could be that these *grammata* contained some divine revelation about the prohibition of the beans: cf. Frazer's *Pausanias*, IV 240. On ἱερὸς λόγος see also Hdt. II 81 (about the prohibition of wool, common to Egyptians, Orphics, and Pythagoreans: cf. I. M. Linforth, *The Arts of Orpheus*, 38 ff.): ἔστι δὲ περὶ αὐτῶν ἱρὸς λόγος λεγόμενος, and Plato, *Ep.* VII 335A 2 (about the punishments in the Afterworld): πείθεσθαι δὲ ὄντως ἀεὶ χρὴ τοῖς παλαιοῖς τε καὶ ἱεροῖς λόγοις.

⁵ These revelations are said, XLVII 1 (376.5 Keil), to be τὰ τοῦ Σωτῆρος ἀγωνίσματα ("sc. *studia et facinora*," Keil), and they are, in fact, achievements or miracles of Asclepius. Thus Aristides' *Sacred Stories* could be classed in the Hellenistic γένος of aretalogies; upon this cf. R. Reitzenstein, *Hellenistische Wundererzählungen* (Berlin, 1906) 1–99. The title ἱεροὶ λόγοι has the approbation of the god himself in XLVIII 9 (396.30 Keil).

⁶ The date is Boulanger's (461 ff.: see head note *supra*), taken over by Wilamowitz without even a mention of Schmid's date (p. 129 in Schmid-Stählin). On Hadrianutherae cf. Wilamowitz 333 ("75 Kilometer südlich von Kyzikos"); also 334: "seine Kindheit gehört nach Mysien, und zwar in eine Gegend, die nicht nach der Äolis, sondern nach Kyzikos gravitierte."

⁷ XLVIII 60 K.; cf. L 2 K. The Aesepus, to which reference is made in Homer (*Il.* 12.21), today Goenen Tchaï, falls into the Propontis, and forms the boundary between Troas and Mysia: *P.-W.* 1085.

⁸ φάρμακα δὲ θήρειά τε καὶ ἄλλα παντοῖα : θήρεια φάρμακα seems to be the

same as θηριακὰ φάρμακα, which designates a sort of antidote in ancient medicine.

9 On the illnesses of Aristides, see also XLIX 16–21 K.: description of a new illness, Aristides being at home at Hadrianutherae *ca.* 166, some twenty years after the first departure for Pergamum.

10 M. Wellmann, *Fragmenta der Sikelischen Ärzte*, p. 50.

11 Plato, *Leg.* I (633c): χειμώνων ἀνυποδησίαι.

12 Aristopho Comicus (IV b.c.) 10, 8 Kock (8, 8 Bothe).

13 ἀνυπόδητον περιπατεῖν, Dittenberger, *Sylloge*, 3d ed., inscr. 1170, 11 f. (Edelstein 432).

14 Galen *de san. tuenda* I 8, 19–21 (Edelstein 413).

15 Edelstein 317 (p. 161).

16 καὶ λούειν ψυχρῷ, θέρμης, οὐδ' ὅλως ⟨ψύχους⟩, ὡς ἄν τις δόξαι, δεόμενον (ψύχους addidi: θέρμης, οὐ ψύχους iam Dindorf).

17 For other passages where Aristides emphasizes the παράδοξον of Asclepius cures, cf. XLVIII 59 and 73 K.

18 ὑποδήματα Αἰγύπτια. Shoes of linen, not of leather, in accordance with a well-known taboo on leather in shrines (cf. A. D. Nock, *CP* XLV [1950] 49, 32)? Or shoes of a certain form, sc. not sandals but really shoes covering the whole foot with only the toes left bare, as represented in some "Shoes of Sarapis" (for example, S. Dow, *Harv. Theol. Rev.* XXX [1937] 225 and fig. 3)? Or sandals made of palm leaves, as the soleae of Isis (Apul. *Met.* XI 4, 3: pedes ambroseos tegebant *soleae palmae victricis foliis intextae*) or the baxeae of the Egyptian prophet Zatchlas (*ibid.* II 28, 2: iuvenem quempiam linteis amiculis iniectum *pedesque palmeis baxeis inductum*)? Palm twigs and palm leaves are a symbol of immortality; cf. W. Wittman, *op. cit.* (chap. v, head note) 51 f. with reference to the use of βαïs in Horapollo I 7 and the magical papyri.

19 For the passage from "I was ordered" onward, cf. Edelstein 408.

20 Perhaps a distribution of corn. Cf. L. and S. (Jones) s.v., I.

21 For the description of other cold baths cf. XLVIII 45 ff. (404.26 ff. K.). Bath at Pergamum in the Caicus, XLVIII 46–49 K. Bath at Smyrna, XLVIII 50 K. Bath at Pergamum in the Selinus (Keil ad 406.2; cf. 400.23), XLVIII 51–53 K. Bath in the sea at Elaea (harbor of Pergamum), XLVIII 54–59 K.

22 The tricephalic hound of Hades, Cerberus, generally figured with Sarapis, who is a chthonian deity. But Aristides sometimes confuses

the two gods (cf. XLIX 47 K.: Asclepius and Sarapis τινα τρόπον ἀλλήλοις ἐμφερεῖς); Asclepius is associated with Sarapis and Isis at Aegira of Achaia (Pausanias VII 26, 7 and Edelstein 672); he has the dog as an attribute (Edelstein 630, 691, and II 227 f.), and dogs cure the patients at Epidaurus by licking them (Edelstein 423, 26). On the symbolism of the three heads of Cerberus, cf. Macrobius *Sat.* I 20, 3 (past, present, future) and Pettazzoni, *Mélanges Picard* (1949) II, 803 ff.

[23] ἐξεβόησα· Εἶς, λέγων δὴ τὸν θεόν (428.32 K.). This is the liturgical εἶς θεός acclamation, for which cf. E. Peterson Εἶς Θεός (Göttingen, 1926). Asclepius' answer σὺ εἶ means that Aristides, for his part, is the εἶς among all orators.

[24] On this passage cf. Edelstein, I, 302 and II, 107 f.

[25] XLIX 46–48 K. (Edelstein 325).

[26] *Asclepius*, II, 129 and n. 15.

[27] "consciousness . . . presence": καὶ γνώμης ὄγκος ἀνεπαχθής (obscure!). For εἰ δέ τις τῶν τετελεσμένων ἐστίν, σύνοιδέν τε καὶ γνωρίζει (p. 402.3 K. and 474 D.), cf. XLVIII 28 K.: "After that (sc. after a special kindness of Asclepius), one can well imagine what were my feelings and how strongly, for my part, I was bound to the god. As in an initiation (ὥσπερ ἐν τελετῇ, 401.4 K.), I was nearly always considering all those things, afraid and at the same time full of high hopes." This allusion to a *telete* seems to me purely metaphorical (like XXIII 16, 36.1 ff. K., XLII 520, 773 D., Edelstein 402: εἰς Ἀσκληπιοῦ τε συμφοιτῆσαι καὶ τελεσθῆναι τὰ πρῶτα τῶν ἱερῶν ὑπὸ τῷ καλλίστῳ καὶ τελεωτάτῳ δᾳδούχῳ καὶ μυσταγωγῷ). As Edelstein says (II, 129, 15): "The true mysteries of Asclepius, in the opinion of Aristides, were his healings. . . . It seems that the Greek Asclepius . . . did not reveal mysteries."

[28] *Loc. cit.* (head note *supra*) 338–340.

[29] XLIII 30 K. (I 8, p. 11 D.): οὗτος (Zeus) . . . ἐν δὲ νόσοις καὶ πᾶσιν καιροῖς βοηθῶν Σωτήρ.

[30] XLIII 25 K. (I 7, p. 9 D.): Ἀσκληπιὸς ἰᾶται οὓς ἰᾶσθαι Διὶ φίλτερον. Later, on the contrary, Asclepius will be considered as having the same power as Zeus: cf. XLII 4, p. 335.11 ff. K. (VI 37, p. 65 D.) with the correction of Wilamowitz (*loc. cit.* [head note *supra*] 345, 1): εἰ δ' Ἀπόλλωνος παῖδα καὶ τρίτον ἀπὸ Διὸς νομίζομεν αὐτόν (Asclepius), αὖθις αὐ⟨τὼ⟩ (Wil.: αὖ codd.) καὶ συνάπτομεν τοῖς ὀνόμασιν (temple of Zeus Asclepius at Pergamum, 335.5 K., cf.

XLVII 45, 78 K.; L 46 K. [VI 37, p. 64 D.]), ἐπεί τοι καὶ αὐτὸν τὸν Δία γενέσθαι λέγουσίν ποτε, πάλιν δὲ αὐτὸν (Zeus) ἀποφαίνουσιν ὄντα τῶν ὄντων πατέρα καὶ ποιήτην. Now of Asclepius it has been said 335.8 K. (p. 64 D.) : οὗτός ἐσθ᾽ ὁ τὸ πᾶν ἄγων καὶ νέμων σωτὴρ τῶν ὅλων καὶ φύλαξ τῶν ἀθανάτων ..., σῴζων τά τε ὄντα καὶ τὰ γιγνόμενα. See also L 45 K. on offerings to Asclepius ὡς δὴ Διί.

31 XLV 13 K. (VIII 50, p. 87 D.) : εὐχὴν ἀποπληροῦντας ἐπειδήπερ ἐσώθημεν, 33; cf. Wilamowitz (as mentioned in head note *supra*) 339.

32 Cf. note 22 *supra*.

33 XLV 18 K. (VIII 52, p. 89 D.) : τὸ δὲ σῶμα ὑγίειαν διδοὺς σῴζει, and XLV 34 K. (VIII 56, p. 97 D.) : τὰ νῦν μὴ πρόες με, ἀλλ᾽ ἀνάσωσον. Cf. A. Höfler, *Der Sarapishymnus des Ailios Aristeides*, Tübinger Beiträge 27 (Stuttgart, 1935) 46 ff., 71 ff.

34 Rome XLVIII 63 (409.4 K.) : καὶ οἱ ἰατροὶ καθάρσεις προσῆγον, (409.7) καὶ τέλος οἱ ἰατροί. Smyrna XLVIII 69 (410.17 K.) : καὶ συνῆλθον οἵ τε ἰατροὶ καὶ γυμνασταί.

35 Rome XLVIII 64 K.: καὶ τί χρὴ ποιεῖν οὐκ ἦν. Smyrna XLVIII 69 K.: οὔτε βοηθεῖν εἶχον οὔτε ἐγνώριζον τὴν ποικιλίαν τῆς νόσου.

36 XLVIII 7 K.: εἴ τι δυναίμην γενέσθαι ῥᾴων.

37 XLVIII 7 K.: ἐνταῦθα πρῶτον ὁ Σωτὴρ χρηματίζειν ἤρξατο.

38 In addition to Pergamum (Edelstein 801–812), Asclepius had sanctuaries at Nicomedia (*ibid.* 800), Lampsacus (572), Smyrna (813–814: it was a foundation of the sanctuary of Pergamum, 709), Ephesus (573), Tralles (815), Aegae (816–820).

39 Cf. in the inscriptions of the Tiberine Island the formula ἀφηλπισμένῳ ὑπὸ παντὸς ἀνθρώπου, Dittenberger, *Sylloge*, 3d ed., 1173.7, 11 (Edelstein 438), and *Pap. Oxyrh.* 1381, col. III, 54 ff. πολλάκις ἀπηυδηκυίης τῆς ἰατρικῆς πρὸς τὰς κατεχούσας αὐτοὺς νόσους ἔσωσεν (sc. Asclepius-Imouthes). It is a common topic; cf. Edelstein 404, 422, 582, 585.

40 XLVIII 7 (396.12 K.): καὶ ἐβόων δὴ ἐν τῷ ὀνείρατι ὡς ἂν ὕπαρ τε καὶ ἐπ᾽ ὀνείρατι τετελεσμένῳ· 'μέγας ὁ Ἀσκληπιός.' Cf. XLVIII 21 (399.22 f., K.): ὡς δ᾽ ἐξέβην, ... βοὴ πολλὴ τῶν τε παρόντων καὶ ἐπιόντων, τὸ πολυύμνητον δὴ τοῦτο βοώντων 'μέγας ὁ Ἀσκληπιός,' and E. Peterson (*op. cit.* in n. 23 *supra*) 196 ff., 206.

41 See also L 102 K. The people of Smyrna want to give to Aristides the priesthood of Asclepius, but he says that οὐδὲν οὔτε μεῖζον οὔτε ἔλαττον οἷόν τ᾽ εἴη πράττειν μοι ἄνευ τοῦ θεοῦ, οὐδ᾽ οὖν αὐτὸ τὸ ἱερᾶσθαι νομίζειν ἐξεῖναι πρότερον πρὶν ἂν αὐτοῦ πίθωμαι τοῦ θεοῦ.

42 *Onirocr.* II 25, p. 120.7 Hercher.

NOTES TO CHAPTER VII
Reflective Piety
Man and the World
(Pages 105–121)

1 *Liberté et civilisation chez les Grecs* (Paris, Editions de la Revue des Jeunes, 1947) 65 ff.

2 W. Chase Greene, *Moira, Fate, Good and Evil in Greek Thought* (Harvard Univ. Press, 1944). Cf. my review of this work in *Rev. de Philologie* XXII (1948) 147 ff.

3 Epictetus I 16, 16 and 20.

4 Translation by Michael Balkwill, No. 483 in Higham and Bowra, eds., *The Oxford Book of Greek Verse in Translation* (1938).

5 Cf. already Heraclitus, fr. 102 D.: τῷ μὲν θεῷ καλὰ πάντα καὶ ἀγαθὰ καὶ δίκαια, ἄνθρωποι δὲ ἃ μὲν ἄδικα ὑπειλήφασιν ἃ δὲ δίκαια.

6 Cf. the subscriptions of book I, τὰ ἐν Κουάδοις πρὸς τῷ Γρανούᾳ, and of book II, τὰ ἐν Καρνούντῳ.

7 All the quotations of Marcus Aurelius are from A. S. L. Farquharson, *The Meditations of the Emperor Marcus Antoninus*, Vol. I (Oxford, 1944), sometimes slightly modified.

8 Cf. in the present volume chap. vi, p. 91.

9 See also II 4, 2; II 9.

10 See also II 17, 4.

11 V 27, 2: ὁ ἑκάστου νοῦς καὶ λόγος.

12 See also VI 30, 4; III 6.2; VI 7, etc.

13 II 5, 1: τὸ ἐν χερσί.

14 *Stoicorum Veterum Fragmenta*, Index, 92 col. II; Cleanthes, the Hymn to Zeus, 12.

15 Cf. E. Peterson, *Der Monotheismus als politisches Problem* (Leipzig, 1935) 50 ff., esp. 52. (In 51, last line, and 52, 1.5, correct "Philostrat" to "Apollonios von Tyana," and in 52, 1.23 add ἀξίωμα after τὸ γὰρ μέγιστον). Already Xenophanes, fr. 23 D., εἷς θεός, ἔν τε θεοῖσι καὶ ἀνθρώποισι μέγιστος. This is definitely not "ein radikaler Monotheismus," as scholars since Wilamowitz have got into the habit of saying.

16 Peterson, *op. cit.* (in last preceding note) 25 ff., 108 ff., 126 f.

17 *Stoicorum Vet. Fr.* III, Nos. 333–339.

[18] F. Cumont, "Le Mysticisme astral dans l'antiquité," *Bull. Acad. Roy. de Belgique* (Classe de Lettres) 5 (1919) 256 ff.

[19] Julian, *Or.* IV (*Hymn to King Helios*) 130. I have availed myself of the translation of Wilmer Cave Wright, *Julian* I 353 ff. (*L.C.L.*).

[20] Cf. *The Oxford Book of Greek Verse in Translation*, No. 621. On this epigram, the best study is that of F. Boll, "Das Epigramm des Claudius Ptolemaeus," *Sokrates* IX (1921) 2 ff.; republished in *Kleine Schriften* (Leipzig, Koehler u. Amelang, 1950) 143 ff.

[21] "The authorship is not certain. It seems to be a folksong." *Oxford Book* . . . , No. 696). Cf. also Wilamowitz, *Textgeschichte der griechischen Lyriker* (Berlin, 1900) 33, 1; also his *Sappho und Simonides* (Berlin, 1913) 75, 1.

[22] Translation by J. M. Edmonds, *Oxford Book* . . . , No. 156. I cannot refrain from quoting also the lovely imitation by A. E. Housman, *The Collected Poems* (London, 1939) 170:

The rainy Pleiads wester,	The rainy Pleiads wester,
Orion plunges prone,	And seek beyond the sea
The stroke of midnight ceases,	The head that I shall dream of
And I lie down alone.	That shall not dream of me.

[23] Aesch. *Agam.* 16–19. The translation is Gilbert Murray's (Oxford, 1920), as in what follows, except that in verse 1 for θεοὺς μὲν αἰτῶ I write "the gods" in place of "God."

[24] *Agam.* vv. 1–6, bracketing v. 7. Gilbert Murray, as also Professor Ed. Fraenkel, the latest editor of the *Agamemnon*, rejects v. 7.

[25] Cf. Schmid, I 3 (1940) 639–641.

[26] Cf. Fraenkel's edition of the *Agamemnon* (Oxford, 1950) II, 187, 1. According to Fraenkel, the *Andromeda* of Euripides also began with an anapestic prologue.

[27] Eurip. *Iph. Aulid.* 6–11, in Murray's translation, slightly modified. I give all of 6–11 to Agamemnon and read therefore, v. 7, σείριος, "brilliant star," not the star Sirius.

[28] In the *Ausgabe von 1789.* Written "am Hang des Ettersberg, den 12. Februar 76."

[29] The change of feeling between archaic Greek poetry and Ptolemy is very interesting from another point of view also. It was a Greek conviction, firmly implanted from of old, that man must not try to become a god. So already Alcman, *Parthen.* 16 ff.: [μή] τις ἀνθ]ρώπων ἐς ὠρανὸν ποτήσθω / [μηδὲ πει]ρήτω γαμῆν τὴν 'Αφροδίταν. Pindar never

grows tired of impressing this advice on the minds of the young prizewinners in the Greek games, e.g., *Isthm.* VII 43 ff.: τὰ μακρὰ δ' εἴ τις / παπταίνει, βραχὺς ἐξικέσθαι χαλκόπεδον θεῶν ἕδραν· ὅτι πτερόεις ἔρριψε Πάγασος / δεσπόταν ἐθέλοντ' ἐς οὐρανοῦ σταθμοὺς / ἐλθεῖν μεθ' ὁμάγυριν Βελλεροφόνταν Ζηνός, and *Isthm.* V 14 ff.: μὴ μάτευε Ζεὺς γενέσθαι ... (16) θνατὰ θνατοῖσι πρέπει. To give a concluding example, this is also the original significance of the story of Diagoras of Rhodes on which Cicero expatiates after the rationalist fashion of his time in the *Tusculan Disputations,* I 46, 110 ff.: Secundis vero suis rebus volet etiam mori (sc. the wise man); non enim tam cumulus bonorum iucundus esse potest quam molesta decessio. (111) Hanc sententiam significare videtur Laconis illa vox, qui, cum Rhodius Diagoras, Olympionices nobilis, uno die duo suos filios victores Olympiae vidisset, accessit ad senem et gratulatus, "Morere, Diagora," inquit, "non enim in caelum ascensurus es." (The original meaning is given by Pindar in his ode for Diagoras himself, *Olymp.* VII 90, ἐπεὶ ὕβριος ἐχθρὰν ὁδὸν εὐθυπορεῖ, or in *Pyth.* X 27, where, after praising the man who, once crowned victor himself, sees his son winning a crown also, he writes: ὁ χάλκεος οὐρανὸς οὔ ποτ' ἀμβατὸς αὐτῷ.)

Now, on the contrary, Ptolemy says οὐκέτ' ἐπιψαύω γαίης ποσίν, ἀλλὰ παρ' αὐτῷ / Ζανὶ θεοτρεφέος πίμπλαμαι ἀμβροσίης. Yet it cannot be maintained that Ptolemy is un-Greek, nor can it be supposed, for example, that this new attitude may have been imported from the Orient; for Ptolemy, in his astronomical and even in his astrological writings, shows himself an exponent of the Greek manner of thinking. This tremendous change developed from within Greek thought itself, and, fundamentally, we may consider Plato to have been its first cause.

NOTES TO CHAPTER VIII

Reflective Piety
The Contemplation of God
(Pages 122–139)

[1] Cf. Archimandrite Spiridon, *Mes Missions en Sibérie: Souvenirs d'un moine orthodoxe russe,* trans. Pierre Pascal (Paris, 1950), pp. 13 ff.

[2] Albinus, *Didaskalikos* 4, 2 (154.18 Hermann): διττὸς δ' ἐστιν ὁ λόγος·

ὁ μὲν γάρ ἐστι παντελῶς ἄληπτός τε καὶ ἀτρεκής, ὁ δὲ κατὰ τὴν τῶν πραγμάτων γνῶσιν ἀδιάψευστος, τούτων δὲ ὁ μὲν πρότερος θεῷ δυνατός, ἀνθρώπῳ
δὲ ἀδύνατος.

3 *Didask.* 9, 1 (163.13 H.).

4 *Ibid.* 9, 2 (163.27 H.); 9, 3 (163.29 ff. H.).

5 Plato, *Symposium* 210E ff. For the negative formulation (οὔτε . . .
οὔτε etc.) cf. already Parmenides, fr. 8.22 ff. D., and see also Albinus
in the text of this present chapter, p. 128. For the end (ἀλλὰ αὐτὸ
καθ᾽ αὐτὸ μεθ᾽ αὐτοῦ μονοειδὲς ἀεὶ ὄν, 211B 1) cf. Parmenides 8.29:
ταὐτόν τ᾽ ἐν ταὐτῷ τε μένον καθ᾽ ἑαυτό τε κεῖται.

6 *Contemplation . . . selon Platon*, 2d ed. (Paris, 1950) 228 ff.

7 *Didask.* 10, 1 (164.6 H.).

8 The two others are Matter and Ideas; cf. 9, 1 (163.10 H.).

9 *Didask.* 10, 3 (164.27 H.).

10 *Ibid.* 10, 4 (165.4 ff.).

11 ἀδιάφορον legi: διαφορά, codd. Cf. my *Révélation d'Hermès Trismégiste*
(Paris, 1948) II, 92, 1.

12 Reading with P οὐ γὰρ ἐστέρηται τοῦ ποιὸν εἶναι ἐπιβάλλοντος εἶναι
αὐτῷ᾽ποιῷ (ποιῷ αὐτῷ P, correxi).

13 ἀνεκλάλητε, ἄρρητε, σιωπῇ φωνούμενε *Corp. Herm.* I 31 (19.2). For the
Hermetica I have used the translation of W. Scott, with some modi-
fications, however, where he has introduced changes into the text.

14 *Corp. Herm.* X 5 (115.12 ff.). Many other texts are quoted by O.
Casel, "De Silentio Mystico Philosophorum Graecorum," *Religions-
geschichtliche Versuche und Vorarbeiten* (1919) No. 2.

15 Cf. Albinus, e.g., *Didask.* 10, 3 (164.24 ff. H.).

16 On this subject I still maintain the interpretation which I gave in
Rév. Herm. Trism. II, 117 ff., notwithstanding the criticism offered
by Professor Harold Cherniss in *Gnomon* (1950) 207 ff. Cf. the
Preface to the third volume of *Rév. Herm. Trism.*

17 *Corp. Herm.* IV 4.

18 *Ibid.* IX 4.

19 In *Symposium* 210D.

20 Cf. Ζωὴ καὶ φῶς *Corp. Herm.* I 9, 12, and τὸ λαμπρὸν φῶς *ibid.* VII, 2.
Cf. also G. P. Wetter, *Phôs* (Uppsala, 1915), and R. Bultmann,
"Zur Geschichte der Lichtsymbolik im Altertum," *Philologus*
XCVII (1948) 1 ff.

21 Bultmann, *loc. cit.* 35.

22 *de Mut. nom.* 7 (III 157, 11 C.-W.).

[23] *Corp. Herm.* X 4 (114.19): Ἐπλήρωσας ἡμᾶς, ὦ πάτερ, τῆς ἀγαθῆς καὶ καλλίστης θέας καὶ ὀλίγου δεῖν ἐσβέσθη μου ὁ τοῦ νοῦ ὀφθαλμὸς ὑπὸ τῆς τοιαύτης θέας. The codd. have the unintelligible ἐσεβάσθη: ἐπεσκιάσθη, Scott ("blinded"), ἐπετάσθη Reitzenstein. (Professor Nock now thinks ἐσεβάσθη possible with the meaning "was hallowed.")

[24] Numenius, fr. 11 Leemans (Brussels, 1937).

[25] τούτων τῶν ἐπακτρίδων τῶν †μόνων†, 131.8 Leemans. Corruptum; μονοκώπων ci. Usener.

[26] Cf. E. Peterson, "Herkunft und Bedeutung der ΜΟΝΟΣ ΠΡΟΣ ΜΟΝΟΝ—Formel bei Plotin," *Philologus* LXXXVIII (1932) 30 ff.

[27] The translation is from F. M. Cornford's *Plato's Cosmology*, 2d ed., p. 353.

Index

INDEX

Ancient Authors Quoted

SUBJECTS

Anachoresis. See Retirement

Apotattesthai, 155 n. 22

Apuleius, *Metamorphoses* XI, 68–84 (chap. v); as autobiography, 76 f., 163 n. 33; bibliography of, 158; Fortune in, 74 f., 162 nn. 26, 27; Isis in, *see* Isis; Lucius in, *see* Lucius; mysteries in, 71 f., 160 nn. 18–21; rebirth in, 78, 164 n. 45; relation with other books, 72, 161 n. 22; words and phrases in: *ara Misericordiae,* 160 n. 11; *castimoniae,* 162 n. 32; *dignatio,* 78, 164 n. 44; *monitus,* 78, 164 n. 43, *portus Quietis,* 160 n. 11; *religiosa cohors,* 165 n. 52; *sancta militia,* 165 n. 52; *servitium,* 80, 165 n. 52

Aretalogies of Isis, 41, 151 n. 5, 162 n. 28

Aristides, Aelius: bibliography of, 166 f.; dream-visions of, 95 ff.; illnesses of, 88 ff., 92 f., 169 n. 9; treatments of, 91 ff. (cold baths, 91, 94 f., 169 n. 21; Egyptian shoes, 93, 169 n. 18; paradoxical, 92, 169; riding horseback, 91, 93 f.; walking barefoot, 91 f., 93, 169 nn. 11, 12); works of, 167 n. 1; meaning of *Hieroi Logoi,* 88, 168 n. 4

Artemis and Hippolytus, 11 ff.

Asclepius: and Aristides, 94 ff.; and Sarapis, 97, 169 n. 22; and Zeus, 170 n. 30; as the World-Soul, 96 f.; acclamations of, 90, 95, 96, 170 n. 23; epiphanies of, 88

Athena: and Athens, 37 f.; and Heracles, 7; and Theseus, 6; Attic offerings to, 6, 143 n. 1

Aurelius, Marcus, 112 ff.

Christian piety, 3 ff., 7 f., 38 f., 144 n. 15

Contemplation: of the Cosmos, 117 ff.; in Archimandrite Spiridon, 122 f., 174 n. 1; in Cleanthes, 111 f.; in Julian, 118, 173 n. 19; in Marcus Aurelius, 112 ff.; in Plato, 45 ff.; in late theology, 134
  of the divine Intellect, 135 ff.
  of the Night, 119 ff., 122; Sappho's song, 119; Ptolemy's epigram, 118; Goethe's *Nachtlied,* 120
  of the "Unknown God": in Plato, 42 ff.; in Numenius, 138; in late theology, 134

Cosmos: optimistic view of the, 130 f.; pessimistic view of the, 131 ff. *See also* Contemplation

Fortune (Tyche): in the Hellenistic Age, 41; against Lucius, 73 f.; Isis as, 74 f.

God: idea of, 5, 143 n. 3, justice of, 34 f.; the Unknown, 128 ff.

Gods: and men, 20 ff.; and the Blessed, 23 ff., 148 nn. 16, 17; three, 129 f.; as Saviors, 41

Hellenistic Age, religious changes in the, 39 ff.

Hippolytus: age of, 145; *aidos* of, 13, 146 f. nn. 20-25; legend of, 10 f., 146 n. 19; prayer of, 12; purity of, 11, 13, 145 n. 19; sin of, 145 f. n. 19

Isis: aretalogies of, 41, 151 n. 5, 162 n. 28; ass loathsome to, 158 n. 22; contemplation of, 80 ff.; daily cult of, 81, 165 n. 54; discourse of, 159 n. 6; orders of, 77 ff., 163 nn. 39, 41, 164 nn. 42, 43

Lucius: as Apuleius, 76 f., 163 nn. 33-37; character of, 76, 162 n. 31; conversion of, 75 f.; *curiositas* of, 75, 162 n. 29; dream-visions of, 79; initiations of, 71 f.; prayer to the Moon, 69, 158 n. 4; prayers to Isis, 81 f., 162 n. 27, 166 n. 56; story of, 68 ff.; vocation of, 77 ff., 163 n. 40, 165 nn. 48, 49

185

CPSIA information can be obtained at www.ICGtesting.com
Printed in the USA
BVOW011516120613

323107BV00011B/670/P

9 781258 152734